Preventing Crime

Rick Sarre

Preventing Crime

What We Know, and What We Need to Do

Rick Sarre
Justice and Society
University of South Australia
Adelaide, SA, Australia

ISBN 978-981-97-3487-0   ISBN 978-981-97-3488-7 (eBook)
https://doi.org/10.1007/978-981-97-3488-7

© The Editor(s) (if applicable) and The Author(s), under exclusive license to Springer Nature Singapore Pte Ltd. 2024

This work is subject to copyright. All rights are solely and exclusively licensed by the Publisher, whether the whole or part of the material is concerned, specifically the rights of translation, reprinting, reuse of illustrations, recitation, broadcasting, reproduction on microfilms or in any other physical way, and transmission or information storage and retrieval, electronic adaptation, computer software, or by similar or dissimilar methodology now known or hereafter developed.
The use of general descriptive names, registered names, trademarks, service marks, etc. in this publication does not imply, even in the absence of a specific statement, that such names are exempt from the relevant protective laws and regulations and therefore free for general use.
The publisher, the authors and the editors are safe to assume that the advice and information in this book are believed to be true and accurate at the date of publication. Neither the publisher nor the authors or the editors give a warranty, expressed or implied, with respect to the material contained herein or for any errors or omissions that may have been made. The publisher remains neutral with regard to jurisdictional claims in published maps and institutional affiliations.

Cover illustration: © Melisa Hasan

This Palgrave Macmillan imprint is published by the registered company Springer Nature Singapore Pte Ltd.
The registered company address is: 152 Beach Road, #21-01/04 Gateway East, Singapore 189721, Singapore

If disposing of this product, please recycle the paper.

This book is dedicated to my late parents, Brian Robert Sarre (1927–2022) and Winifred Grace Turner Sarre (1931–2004) who gave me the educational opportunities I was fortunate to enjoy, both in Australia and in North America.

This book is also dedicated to the memory of sociolegal polymath the late Professor Roman Tomasic, a long-term colleague and friend. On July 14, 2022, I attended his funeral. His legacy, fortunately, lives on in the pages of the journals to which he contributed, in the words in the books he wrote, and in the lives of the students he taught.

Finally, I dedicate this work to the thousands of men and women in Australia who give their time professionally and voluntarily to the task of crime prevention. Bodies such as the Australian Crime Prevention Council (led by Auxiliary Judge and a former Master of the South Australian Supreme Court, Peter Norman) typify these organisations. These groups are committed to reducing victimisation in a range of ways. Their work is mostly unheralded, yet provides a valuable and ongoing service to the community. They deserve our praise.

Foreword

At a time where media headlines often scream the latest crime statistics or sensationalised criminal acts, it is easy to overlook the quieter, more subtle mechanisms that shape our society's relationship with crime.

This book delves into a realm less explored, yet equally vital: social crime prevention. In our, sometimes desperate, attempt to combat crime, we often focus on reactive measures—police patrols, judicial proceedings, and incarceration strategies. However, amidst the ongoing, resounding, clamour for security measures, there exists a profound truth often overlooked: true safety and security are not merely the absence of crime but the presence of trust, equality of opportunity, and robust social capital. This book illuminates this truth with the conviction that the author is known for. Tucked away in our communities lies a potent force. Social crime prevention is the collective effort of individuals, families, educators, community leaders, and policymakers to address the root causes of crime before they sprout into criminal behaviour.

This book shines a spotlight on the less obvious yet profoundly impactful strategies for preventing crime. It underscores that crime prevention is not solely the responsibility of law enforcement and the judicial system; rather, it is a duty that is shared by every member of society. From nurturing supportive family environments to fostering inclusive communities, from providing access to food, housing, quality education, and employment opportunities to addressing socio-economic inequalities, every action contributes to the intricate tapestry of crime prevention.

Drawing from the evidence, Rick Sarre's book justly argues that a safe and secure community is one founded on principles of trust, equality, and social investment. It articulates how the development of strong social capital and the investment in constructive pathways can reshape lives and fortify communities against crime. However, it also warns against the pitfalls of shortsighted spending cuts in crime prevention, cautioning that hastily bolstering police and prisons may compromise long-term safety and exacerbate societal inequalities.

In the Australian context, navigating the landscape of crime prevention presents unique challenges. The division of labour among government entities, with policing, prosecutions, courts, and corrections mostly falling under the purview of states and territories, exemplifies the need for a multi-level approach. While federal intervention is pivotal in addressing transnational crimes, much of the pain experienced by victims remains localized, demanding tailored local initiatives for effective prevention.

Indeed, the aphorism holds true: to prevent crime, we must shape our communities to discourage crime and intervene early in the lives of those at risk of entanglement in the justice system. This means not only addressing individual needs but also nurturing the socio-economic and cultural fabric of our society.

Over the past half-century, a wealth of research has documented and emphasised effective crime prevention strategies. Yet, the challenge lies not in the lack of knowledge but in its implementation. Effective policy-making demands well-informed debates free from the shackles of political rhetoric. This book serves as a beacon, signalling policymakers and citizens alike with the knowledge needed to navigate the complex terrain of crime prevention.

Over the past half-century, too, a raft of effective crime prevention strategies have been shown, time and time again, to work in various areas of our communities, focusing on a wide range of vulnerabilities, and social determinants of health and well-being. From Australia to Europe, Canada to New Zealand, South Africa to South America and Asia, the literature is already more than compelling. These initiatives have been documented, analysed, and scrutinised from multiple angles. Tough on crime should never be equated with soft on crime prevention and social investment.

Rick Sarre rightfully insists upon a long-term perspective necessary for effective social crime prevention. The fruits of these efforts may not be immediately apparent and may take a generation or two to manifest fully. But just as a seed planted today bears fruit tomorrow, investing in social crime prevention today lays the foundation for safer, more resilient communities in the future. From little things, big things grow, as the song goes.

As you journey through the pages of this book, I urge you to consider the profound implications of social crime prevention. Let us not merely treat the symptoms of crime but strive to address its underlying causes, and recognize that crime prevention is not a task relegated solely to the realm of law enforcement. Rather, it should be a collective endeavour that requires the active participation of all members of society.

Ultimately, the message is clear. Crime prevention involves all of us, not just police and judges. It is about building communities where every individual can thrive, where opportunities abound, and where the cycle of crime is broken. Together, let us embark on this crucial journey towards a safer, more just society.

Associate Professor Isabelle
Bartkowiak-Théron, Ph.D.
Director, Tasmanian Institute of Law
Enforcement Studies;
Executive Board Member, Australian
Crime Prevention Council;
Vice President, Global Law
Enforcement and Public
Health Association
University of Tasmania
Hobart, TAS, Australia

Preface

I have long been interested in crime prevention. On my shelves are many books that have 'crime prevention' or 'crime reduction' in the title, among them Shaftoe (2004), Fleming and Wood (2006), Moss and Stephens (2006), Sutton, Cherney and White (2008), Tilley (2012), Welsh and Farrington (2012), Schneider (2015), Prenzler (2017), Petersen and Das (2018), Sutton, Cherney, White and Clancey (2021), and most recently Lab (2023). This interest stemmed from my taking the opportunity to complete a graduate program in criminology at the Centre of Criminology at the University of Toronto four decades ago. At the Centre I was exposed to sociological and political theories that challenged my (then) world view: a world view that told me that crime was caused by aberrant individuals who were best dealt with by legal systems meting out legal sanctions. It soon occurred to me that this view was seriously limited and led, more often than not, to a downward spiral in the lives of those caught up in the justice system (and their families, especially their offspring). Moreover, it did nothing to stem the flow of new 'recruits' to the business of crime. Time and time again my teachers also pointed out to me that the way the law is constructed, written, and enforced must be considered when one is thinking about crime causation and prevention. Focusing on the individuals who had exhibited the criminal conduct in order to limit or forestall criminal conduct was useful and necessary, but not sufficient.

This book presents my ideas concerning what we now need to do to prevent crime. The selection of the topics is not designed to be comprehensive. It is guided by the fields I have studied and in which I have published. It is modelled obliquely on the watershed work from Norval Morris and Gordon Hawkins (referred to me many years ago by my friend Greg Crafter) entitled *The Honest Politicians' Guide to Crime Control* published in the USA in 1970 (and discussed later in this book). Norval Morris (1923–2004) was an Australian-educated US law professor, criminologist, and advocate for criminal justice and mental health reform. Gordon Hawkins (1919–2004) was an Australian criminologist and director of the University of Sydney's Institute of Criminology from 1981 to 1985. More than five decades ago, they set out a range of reform imperatives that they believed would forestall crime and limit the rising crime rate. My ideas are similarly focused, albeit across my own somewhat limited selection of topics. Like the target audience of *The Honest Politicians' Guide to Crime Control*, I, too, want all politicians to read this book.

Pleasingly, there is great news for those people who want information and commentary on the subject of crime and its control: there is currently a wealth of research evidence. The findings emerging from public and private sources, academic work, and doctoral theses are phenomenal. Russell Smith explored the vast panoply of these sources in two recent research volumes (Smith, 2021; 2023). The material emerging from the Australian and New Zealand Society of Criminology expands exponentially each year too. Its 50th anniversary volume of contemporary research (Deckert and Sarre, 2017) runs to over 900 pages. Since 1986 the Australian Institute of Criminology has been producing succinct research reports known as *Trends and issues in crime and criminal justice*. There are almost 700 of these reports on the Institute's website, www.aic.gov.au. In its first fifty years, the Australian Institute of Criminology produced over 1,800 reports and papers, and its library holds over 100,000 items (Smith, 2023). Since 1997, Tony Doob of the Centre of Criminology at the University of Toronto, with the support of the Department of Justice, Canada, has been collating abstracts from published research papers that he deems worthy of circulating more widely in an accessible (website and email) and succinct form. Over a thousand such abstracts have been collated and published under the title *Criminology Highlights*.

The bottom line is that we are now blessed with an enormous range of criminological resources, policy recommendations, and evaluations. And the number is growing by the day.

Despite this cornucopia of peer-reviewed information and evidence, the public (and the people they vote into office) too often retreat to 'solutions' for the crime problem that have been debunked again and again. How is it possible that we can know so much and yet act as if we know nothing? It is time for our policymakers to act upon the evidence rather than simply pander to those with the loudest voices in the community, voices that typically allege that the only way to stop criminal behaviour is to strengthen the state's policing systems, and put more offenders behind bars (and for longer). My modest proposals in this book are designed to challenge this view. I trust that they can be persuasive in the minds of the people who hold the relevant legislative power and executive purse-strings.

A Note on What is Not Under Discussion

There are a number of topics in this book which I am not discussing in any depth. This is not because they are not important; rather, they have not been the focus of my research.

The first topic not under discussion is drugs policy. The topic of illicit drugs (possession, use, and supply) has long been an issue of contention in any discussion around crime prevention around the world (United Nations, 2010). There are strong views for and against decriminalisation (the removal of criminal penalties for the personal use of drugs) and legalisation (the removal of justice attention generally, including penalties for the personal use of drugs and the supply of drugs), views and opinions that vary with the type of drug and the age and vulnerability of its suppliers and users. Currently there are no noises towards legislative legalisation of drugs in Australia. However, since the mid-1980s, changes to laws and practice have led to every State and Territory adopting if not a *de jure* (at law) decriminalisation of some drugs (principally cannabis), certainly a *de facto* decriminalisation. There are countries around the world that have engaged in experiments with legalisation and decriminalisation (for example, Portugal, Spain, Netherlands, Canada, and some States of the USA), preferring approaches based upon harm minimisation and public health priorities. Some studies show little or no evidence of consequential increased consumption and drug abuse. The literature (declaring views for and against) on these experiments is legion. While I had some part to play in the very early evaluations of the watershed moves in South Australia to decriminalise cannabis in 1985 (Sarre, 1990, Sutton and Sarre, 1992), I have not weighed into the evaluations and debates since. I will leave that discussion to others far more qualified than I am on this topic. Readers should follow up with the work of Don Weatherburn (e.g. Weatherburn, 2009; 2014), Caitlin Hughes (e.g. Hughes et al., 2019; Hughes, Chalmers and Bright, 2020), and Alison Ritter (e.g. Ritter, 2022).

Secondly, I do not consider in this book the role of alcohol abuse and addiction in the crime cycle. Other than my observations in Chapter 10 on the subject of studies that recommend restricting the ready availability of alcoholic beverages in selected suburbs, I have not examined in any detail the significant role alcohol plays in crime. Hence, I refer readers instead to the extensive literature on this subject authored by the researchers from the Drug Use Monitoring in Australia (DUMA) project, for example, Josh Sweeney and Jason Payne (2011) and Dan Lubman. Dr Lubman and his colleagues write about, for example, the impact of alcohol and drug use on brain function, and the relationship between substance use, gambling, mental disorder, and crime. Their research is found at https://research.monash.edu/en/persons/dan-lubman. In terms of prevention of anti-social conduct, they have examined the effect of targeted telephone, online, and face-to-face intervention programs within school, primary care, mental health, and drug treatment settings. It should be of no surprise to readers to find that the factors that they maintain reduce drug-related harms in the community are as follows: a focus on support for drug users, on access to treatment, and on early intervention and programs designed to reduce child abuse, maltreatment, and neglect (also Daly, 2014; Lee, 2017; Haslam et al., 2023).

Thirdly, the book has no direct recommendations regarding reducing or eliminating the persistent, appalling, and seemingly unrelenting number of murders perpetrated (usually) by men against their intimate partners, a phenomenon that I was first made aware of more than forty years ago (Wilson, 1983). As this book goes to press, the South Australian government is putting in place a Royal Commission into Domestic, Family, and Sexual Violence. That enquiry is certain to examine the causes of the scourge, and to suggest policy responses. Given that the perpetrators are often likely to take their own lives or are apprehended quickly, one can safely assume that any simple resort to mandating tougher penalties for this crime are not the panacea a lay person might think, or hope. On this subject, readers are referred to the work of a vast array of scholars who have researched extensively family and domestic violence such as Kate Fitz-Gibbon, Sandra Walklate, Jude McCulloch, Jane Maree Maher, Marie Segrave, Dean Wilson, Anastasia Powell, Asher Flynn, and Silke Meyer (see, for example, Fitz-Gibbon et al., 2023; Segrave, Wilson and Fitz-Gibbon, 2017), along with recent empirical research emerging from the Australian Institute of Criminology on the subject of intimate partner femicide (Eriksson, Mazerolle and McPhedran, 2022), and findings regarding the connections between child sexual abuse and violence in intimate relationships (Salter, Woodlock and Dubler, 2023).

Finally, I do not address in any depth the so-called 'situational' crime prevention strategies underpinned by rational choice theory, routine activity theory, crime pattern theory, and the movement that explores crime prevention through environmental design (CPTED). These important perspectives have been championed for decades by researchers such as Ron Clarke, Derek Cornish, Marcus Felson, Richard Wortley, Lorraine Mazerolle, and Patricia and Paul Brantingham, Garner Clancey and Jaap de Waard (see Clarke and Felson, 1993; Cornish and Clarke, 2008; Brantingham and Brantingham, 2008; Wortley and Mazerolle, 2008; Clancey et al., 2018; de Waard, 2022). My interest in crime prevention has more to do with addressing less tangible factors, namely the way in which structuring society and resourcing its public and private social and economic agencies assists in reducing lawlessness. I am less interested in programs, valuable as they are, that 'harden' the targets of criminals and limit the choices of opportunistic offenders.

A Note on Terminology

When one talks about reducing crime, there are many ways that can be expressed, such as 'crime prevention,' 'crime reduction,' 'crime control' and 'deterrence.' All of these terms appear in this book from time to time. The terms 'crime prevention' and 'crime reduction' are preferred, and are presented interchangeably (the latter usefully acknowledging the limits of what can be achieved). I have not, however, eliminated the term 'crime prevention' from my writing because it is the most widely used term in the literature; in some instances, a particular response may have had significant success in eliminating a specific crime. Tim Prenzler, for example, writes about the almost complete demise of automatic teller machine (ATM) robberies over a decade ago following a cleverly conceived and executed multi-party targeted strategy (Prenzler, 2011; Prenzler and Sarre, 2012, pp. 159–162).

A Note on Methodology

Any book such as this needs to offer some reassurance that the methods employed by the cited researchers in reaching their conclusions are sound. I am aware that not every authored piece of research addressing crime prevention is reliable and thus usable. There is a lot of dross in the crime prevention policy literature. In an article I wrote thirty years ago I dealt with the cautions one should take on this subject, detailing which evaluative material is sound, and which is typically not (Sarre, 1994). The reader will need to accept my assurances that the studies that I refer to (there are over 290 research pieces found in the references in this book) have gone through a rigorous peer review process.

A Note on the Implementation of These Ideas

I recognise the difficulties associated with implementation of good policy ideas. I examine in Chapter 9 the perils of the political process, reflecting on an article on this subject that I wrote three decades ago in the context of anti-violence strategies (Sarre, 1991). I can only hope that my recommendations in this book capture the imagination of policymakers who have the courage of their convictions and who are not swayed by ill-informed populism and the untested 'quick fix'.

Adelaide, SA, Australia
February 2024

Rick Sarre

References

Brantingham, P., & Brantingham, P. (2008). Crime Pattern Theory. In R. Wortley & L. Mazerolle (Eds.), *Environmental Criminology and Crime Analysis* (pp. 78–94). Willan.

Clancey, G., Monchuk, L., Anderson, J., & Ellis, J. (2018). Lost in Implementation: NSW Police for Crime Prevention Officer Perspectives on Crime Prevention Through Environmental Design. *Crime Prevention and Community Safety, 20*, 139–153.

Clarke, R. V., & Felson, M. (Eds). (1993). *Routine Activity and Rational Choice: Advances in Criminological Theory 5*. Transaction Publishers.

Cornish, D. B., & Clarke, R. V. (2008). The Rational Choice Perspective. In R. Wortley & L. Mazerolle (Eds.), *Environmental Criminology and Crime Analysis* (pp. 21–47). Willan.

Daly, K. (2014). *Redressing Institutional Abuse of Children*. Palgrave Macmillan.

de Waard, J. (2022). *What Works? A Systematic Overview of Published Meta Evaluations/Synthesis Studies Within the Knowledge Domains of Situational Crime Prevention, Policing, and Criminal Justice Interventions, 1997–2022*. Dutch Ministry of Justice and Security, Law Enforcement Department, Unit for General Crime Policy.

Deckert, A., & Sarre, R. (Eds.). (2017). *The Palgrave Handbook of Australian and New Zealand Criminology, Crime and Justice*. Palgrave Macmillan.

Eriksson, L., Mazerolle, P., & McPhedran, S. (2022). *Giving Voice to the Silenced Victims: A Qualitative Study of Intimate Partner Femicide* (Trends and Issues in Crime and Criminal Justice no. 645). Australian Institute of Criminology.

Fitz-Gibbon, K., Walklate, S., McCulloch, J., & Maher, J. M. (2023). Intimate Femicide/Intimate Partner Femicide. In M. Dawson & S. Mobayed Vega (Eds.), *The Routledge International Handbook on Femicide and Feminicide* (pp. 301–310). Routledge.

Fleming, J., & Wood, J. (Eds.). (2006). *Fighting Crime Together: The Challenges of Policing and Security Networks*. UNSW Press.

Haslam, D., Mathews, B., Pacella, R., Scott, J. G., Finkelhor, D., Higgins, D. J., Meinck, F., Erskine, H. E., Thomas, H. J., Lawrence, D., & Malacova, E. (2023). *The Prevalence and Impact of Child Maltreatment in Australia: Findings from the Australian Child Maltreatment Study: Brief Report*. Queensland University of Technology.

Hughes, C. E., Chalmers, J., & Bright, D. A. (2020). Exploring Interrelationships Between High-level Drug Trafficking and Other Serious and Organised Crime: An Australian Study. *Global Crime, 21*(1), 28–50.

Hughes, C. E., Seear, K., Ritter, A., & Mazerolle, L. (2019). *Criminal Justice Responses Relating to Personal Use and Possession of Illicit Drugs: The Reach of Australian Drug Diversion Programs and Barriers and Facilitators to Expansion* (Drug Policy Modelling Program, Monograph no. 27). National Drug and Alcohol Research Centre, UNSW.

Lab, S. P. (2023). *Crime Prevention: Approaches, Practices, and Evaluations* (11th ed.). Routledge.

Lee, N. (2017, February 14). "Ice Wars" Message Is Overblown and Unhelpful. *The Conversation*. https://theconversation.com/ice-wars-message-is-overblown-and-unhelpful Accessed February 1, 2023.

Moss, K., & Stephens, M. (Eds.). (2006). *Crime Reduction and the Law*. Routledge.

Petersen, D. S., & Das, D. (Eds.). (2018). *Global Perspectives on Crime Prevention and Community Resilience*. Routledge.

Prenzler, T. (2011). Strike Force Piccadilly and ATM Security: A Follow-up Study. *Policing, 5*(3), 236–247.

Prenzler, T. (Ed.). (2017). *Understanding Crime Prevention: The Case Study Approach*. Australian Academic Press.

Prenzler, T., & Sarre, R. (2012). Public-Private Crime Prevention Partnerships. In T. Prenzler (Ed.), *Policing and Security in Practice: Challenges and Achievements* (pp. 149–167). Palgrave Macmillan.

Ritter, A. (2022). *Drug Policy*. Routledge.

Salter, M., Woodlock, D., & Dubler, N. (2023). Secrecy, Control and Violence in Women's Intimate Relationships with Child Sexual Abuse Material Offenders. In R. Brown (Ed.), *Crime and Justice Research 2023* (pp. 162–176). Australian Institute of Criminology.

Sarre, R. (1990). A Review of the Cannabis Expiation Notice Scheme in South Australia. *Australian and New Zealand Journal of Criminology, 23*, 299–303.

Sarre, R. (1991). Political Pragmatism Versus Informed Policy: Issues in the Design, Implementation and Evaluation of Anti-Violence Research and Programs. In D. Chappell, P. Grabosky, & H. Strang (Eds.), *Australian Violence: Contemporary Perspectives* (pp. 263–285). Australian Institute of Criminology.

Sarre, R. (1994). The Evaluation of Criminal Justice Initiatives: Some Observations on Models. *The Journal of Law and Information Science, 5*(1), 35–46.

Schneider, S. (2015). *Crime Prevention: Theory and Practice*. Routledge.

Segrave, M., Wilson, D., & Fitz-Gibbon, K. (2017, January 25). More Police Won't Necessarily Lead to Better Outcomes on Family Violence—Here's What We Need. *The Conversation*. https://theconversation.com/more-police-wont-necessarily-lead-to-better-outcomes-on-family-violence-heres-what-we-need-70755. Accessed January 31, 2024.

Shaftoe, H. (2004). *Crime Prevention: Facts, Fallacies and the Future*. Palgrave Macmillan.

Smith, R. (2021). *The Changing Face of Criminology in Australia and New Zealand*. Sage.

Smith, R. (2023). *Public Sector Criminological Research: The Australian Institute of Criminology 1972–2022*. Palgrave Macmillan.

Sutton, A., & Sarre, R. (1992). Monitoring the South Australian Cannabis Expiation Notice Initiative. *The Journal of Drug Issues, 22*(3), 579–590.

Sutton, A., Cherney, A., & White, R. (2008). *Crime Prevention: Principles, Perspectives and Practices* (1st ed.). Cambridge University Press.

Sutton, A., Cherney, A., White, R., & Clancey, G. (2021). *Crime Prevention, Principles, Perspectives and Practices* (3rd ed.). Cambridge University Press.

Tilley, N. (2012). *Crime Prevention*. Routledge.

United Nations. (2010). *Handbook on the United Nations Crime Prevention Guidelines*. United Nations Office on Drugs and Crime.

Welsh, B. C., & Farrington, D. P. (2012). *The Oxford Handbook on Crime Prevention*. Oxford University Press.

Weatherburn, D. (2009). Dilemmas in Harm Minimization: A Response to My Critics. *Addiction, 104*(3), 335–339.

Weatherburn, D. (2014). The Pros and Cons of Prohibiting Drugs. *Australian and New Zealand Journal of Criminology, 47*(2), 176–189.

Wilson, E. (1983). *What Is to be Done About Violence Against Women?* Pengiun.

Wortley, R., & Mazerolle, L. (Eds.). (2008). *Environmental Criminology and Crime Analysis*. Willan.

Acknowledgements

No work of this nature is possible without the support of first-rate colleagues, and I am exceedingly grateful for the insights of Nicole Moulding, Ben Livings, and Sarah Moulds at the University of South Australia, all of whom have been generous with their time and with their observations on my musings. The Justice and Society Executive Dean, Paula Geldens, continues to offer wonderful support to me even though I am officially retired from the university.

Richard Harding, Adrian Cherney, and Richard Wortley offered comments on a draft that were cogent and illuminating. I am grateful to each of them, too.

My wife Debra has always been supportive of my writing. Our children Millicent and Elliott, both legally trained, are always ready to add a more youthful perspective than I can offer.

I sincerely thank the editors at Palgrave Macmillan who were ready and willing to publish this book as part of their Pivot series.

The opportunity to write a Foreword was accepted eagerly by Isabelle Bartkowiak-Théron, a highly regarded theorist in this field, and I am grateful to her.

I continue to enjoy the collegiality of academics from the Australian and New Zealand Society of Criminology, the University of Adelaide, Flinders University, the University of Toronto, Graceland University, Iowa, the Australian Institute of Criminology, and from my colleagues at Umeå University, Sweden with whom I continue to engage in strong and productive academic relationships.

As ever, I must not forget the late Professor Ingmar Santosh for his inspiration all those years ago.

The author is grateful to the Taylor & Francis Group for their kind permission to reproduce, in part, excerpts from their publications into the chapters of this work as follows:

In Chapter 4

Sarre, R. 'How I would spend $100 million to reduce crime,' *Current Issues in Criminal Justice*, 28(3), 339–353, 2017.
Reproduced with permission of The Licensor through PLSclear.

In Chapter 6

Sarre, R., Brooks, D., Smith, C. & Draper, R. 'Current and Emerging Technologies Employed to Abate Crime and to Promote Security.' In B. Arrigo & H. Bersot (Eds.), *The Routledge Handbook of International Crime and Justice Studies*. Abingdon, Oxon: Routledge, pp. 327–349, 2014.
Reproduced with permission of The Licensor through PLSclear.

In Chapter 7

Sarre, R. 'Gun Control: An Australian Perspective.' In J. Carlson, K. Goss & H. Shapira (Eds.), *Gun Studies: Interdisciplinary Approaches to Politics, Policy, and Practice*. Abingdon, Oxon: Routledge, pp. 177–195, 2019.
Reproduced with permission of The Licensor through PLSclear.

Executive Summary

Governments all over the world are constantly endeavouring to make their communities safer and the lives of their citizens less fearful. For decades now, criminological researchers, challenged to assist in this task, have been asking: 'What is working to reduce crime?' 'What could work better in preventing crime before it erupts?' 'What have we not tried, but could try in the field of crime control?' Pleasingly, the research outputs on this subject are voluminous and growing. From time to time they inform policymaking in productive ways; and this, in turn, has led and will continue to lead to good crime prevention outcomes. But too often the research work is ignored by policymakers. Too often they resort to quick fix justice 'solutions' that do not fix anything, cost an enormous amount, and more often than not make matters worse.

In contrast, this book provides evidence that a safe and secure community is best built on equality of opportunity, and the development of strong social capital and social investments that build and rebuild people's lives in constructive ways. That safety and security can, however, be compromised quickly if the spending choices that we make regarding crime prevention (such as simply shoring up the bulwarks of police and prisons) are poorly thought through. There is an opportunity cost too: every 'crime prevention' dollar that is misspent on an ill-founded 'justice' program is a dollar that could have been spent on a social program that has been shown to be effective.

In its essence, there is a simple aphorism that can be adopted here: if we want to prevent crime, we must focus less on *ex post facto* responses to aberrant behaviour and more on shaping our communities in such a way that crime is less likely to emerge, and to intervene (where that is deemed necessary) early in the lives of those who may be destined to become regular clients of the justice system. This includes not only addressing the needs of specific individuals and groups, but also addressing the social, economic, and cultural milieu in which Australians live.

There is a gnawing political problem in Australia that persists in frustrating much of the useful work in crime prevention, and that is that the division of labour regarding crime control and abatement in Australia is uneven and complicated. Policing, prosecutions, courts, and corrections are all primarily the province of the States and Territories, not the federal government. But in response to corporate crime, international drug crime, cybercrime, child exploitation materials, human trafficking (modern slavery), and terrorism the federal government is required to do the heavy lifting. At the same time, the bulk of the pain experienced by victims is usually local. Crime prevention thus requires a multi-level approach (federal, state, and local), dependent upon the nature of the crime, where it occurs, who the alleged perpetrators are, who the victims are, and the legislated powers available to the relevant enforcement officers.

In the last half a century there has been an enormous amount of research conducted in all of these fields. We now have a very good idea about which strategies can best combat the scourge of crime, protect victims, and stem the tide of young people who keep coming to the attention of police. The challenge for justice policymakers is to employ these strategies and not ignore them. But that can only happen when there are well-informed debates that are free from the politics of law and order. Good policymaking does not happen by chance. It begins with every citizen, indeed, every policymaker and politician, becoming better informed. This book is designed to give its readers that information.

Contents

1	Crime Prevention Defined	1
2	Crime Trends	7
3	Policing and Crime Prevention	15
4	Public/Private Partnerships in Crime Prevention	21
5	Preventing White-Collar Crime	27
6	Surveillance as a Crime Prevention Tool	33
7	Firearms in the Crime Prevention Equation	39
8	Corrections and Crime Prevention	45
9	Avoiding Political Interference in Crime Prevention	55
10	Future Directions Required of All of Us	61
11	My Twelve Imperatives	67
12	Conclusion	71
References		75
Index		97

CHAPTER 1

Crime Prevention Defined

Abstract This chapter looks at the various ways in which crime prevention and crime reduction have been defined in the past and explains why these definitions now need expansion. It then points to the large (and growing) base of valuable research on crime prevention that informs the task, including the databases that exist, the government and private research labs that have been set up, and the multitude of Ph.D. students and other researchers found in criminology and criminal justice departments in Australian universities. These include scholars who have developed and expanded the so-called 'What Works?' literature that has been available to governments for thirty years. The chapter concludes on a despairing note, however, highlighting the inexplicable reluctance of policymakers to be informed by the theoretical and practical research findings (let alone to act upon them), and who regularly fail to rely upon the wealth of evidence found in the available evaluative data.

Keywords Defining crime · Punitive damages · Whole-of-government approaches · Evidence-based research · Policymaking

The classic definition of crime prevention is one crafted over thirty years ago by Jan van Dijk and Jaap de Waard (1991, p. 483) namely, the 'total of all private initiatives and state policies, other than the enforcement

© The Author(s), under exclusive license to Springer Nature Singapore Pte Ltd. 2024
R. Sarre, *Preventing Crime*,
https://doi.org/10.1007/978-981-97-3488-7_1

of the criminal law, aimed at the reduction of damage caused by acts defined as criminal by the state.' Nick Tilley (2012), however, suggests that that definition is deficient, as it excludes the crucial role played by state justice institutions in enforcing the laws that have been put in place to deter, control, or prevent anti-social and criminal behaviour. Tilley's definition, however, is also too narrow. His reference to the criminal law is very useful, but it assumes that the criminal law is a discrete entity, separate from all other branches of the law. This is an untenable distinction. One can think of many ways in which 'criminal-like' law operates to deter conduct but is not criminal law per se. The list of examples is a long one. Considerable punitive damages can be added to a civil judgment in favour of a wronged plaintiff. They are not, strictly speaking, criminal penalties, but they are designed to act as a deterrent. Corporate de-registration (a civil remedy) that shuts a company down can be as much a penalty to a business owner as any financial penalty might be. Moreover, 'banning' orders (affecting corporate directors and business services providers) available to prosecutors and judges under the *Corporations Act* can have a far greater impact on individuals (preventing their income-earning capacity or access to privileges) than any short-term criminal penalty. Enforcement orders under anti-discrimination legislation, and intervention orders applied by police on request from potential domestic violence victims are two more examples of this phenomenon.

Moreover, the van Dijk and de Waard definition does not place sufficient recognition of the partnerships that exist between private security and public law enforcement, preferring to think of these entities as distinct. This is a fallacy (Prenzler & Sarre, 2012, 2014a, 2017). For example, Closed Circuit Television (CCTV) cameras installed by private shopkeepers, designed to deter criminal conduct by capturing images in that precinct, only have a deterrent effect because the institutions of justice (police, prosecution, courts, and corrections) act upon the evidence when the CCTV footage is passed to them. Indeed, if it were not for private persons (either as property owners or through the security personnel they employ) coming to law enforcement authorities with information privately obtained, a great deal of law-breaking would never be prevented, prosecuted, or punished (Draper et al., 2012, pp. 197–200).

Indeed, there is now a long tradition of governments in Australia (at the state and national levels) taking a 'whole-of-government' approach to crime prevention (for example, South Australia, 1989) where crime reductive planning and responses are operationalised in and through a range of ministerial (State and Federal) portfolios such as health, welfare, housing, immigration, ethnic affairs, and education (Clancey, 2020; Clancey et al., 2018; Gant & Grabosky, 2000). In other words, it is not simply in the criminal justice arms of government where the crime prevention thinking needs to be done, and the strategies implemented.

In addition to police and private agencies (and, if a matter is taken forward, prosecutors, judges, and corrections officials) there are citizen services (such as Neighbourhood Watch), local government rangers, information technicians, data collection agents, forensic scientists, security industry personnel, educators, and program evaluators who are regularly involved in the task of crime prevention (Clancey et al., 2016, p. 324; Homel & Fuller, 2015).

This is an important perspective, maintaining that the task of reducing human suffering and victimisation can rarely be handled satisfactorily by governments alone. They are necessary but not sufficient.

That is not to say that everyone agrees with the 'we are all in this together' approach. Sutton et al. (2021), for example, remind us of the importance (from time to time) of segregating some prevention initiatives in order to ensure that one does not taint or get in the way of the other. There are any number of examples where private operatives, for example, have exceeded the bounds of propriety in attempting their own view of a 'just' response (Prenzler & Sarre, 2008a, 2008b).

What does the evidence tell us about the most effective methods of crime prevention? Very simply, it tells us that there are a number of 'levers' that can be manipulated to bring about a reduction in crime. There are levers found in the law (for example, legislated corporate criminal penalties), levers associated with deterrence (for example, policing, security, corrections), levers that address social factors (for example, addressing disparities in health, employment, and education), and levers that manipulate situational factors (for example, CCTV, metadata surveillance, and surveillance technologies). Which levers are available to be pulled, and in what circumstances, are decisions that are made every day in the crime-reductive quest.

The challenge for policymakers is to take the vast panoply of crime prevention research findings and adopt, translate, and implement them in order to get the outcomes sought. This task was addressed introspectively two decades ago in a paper by Richard Harding in which he asserted that a legitimate purpose of criminological research is influencing policy. Based upon an overview of his long career in the field, he remained optimistic that this is possible if the right approach is taken. He concluded as follows:

> There has actually been a dazzling array of effective inputs. ... [I]f the integrity and quality of the research are good enough, and the sense of timeliness and social relevance is acute enough, the criminologist can influence policy whatever his formal position in the overall scheme of things and however he chooses to bring his work to public notice. (Harding, 2003, p. 483)

I have no doubt that Richard Harding is right. We are getting better at commissioning inquiries, interpreting the data, evaluating the programs, and suggesting policy responses that emerge from the data. We now have a large and growing base of good research. By 'good research' I mean evidence-based and data-rich research; reflective research; research that is multidisciplinary; research that engages with those with lived experience; research where the researcher tests and tests again the theoretical assumptions being made; research that is replicable across jurisdictions.

Research findings are manifested in multiple ways. We have significant crime data sets, primarily driven by government crime statistics departments but also by the Australian Bureau of Statistics and the Productivity Commission. The number of journals on criminological topics grows rapidly. Ad hoc papers with preferred policy options are regularly prepared not only by university-based scholars but also by government departments, parliamentary research personnel, and justice practitioners (for example, see Clancey & Lin, 2021; Clancey & Metcalf, 2020; Head et al., 2014; Smith, 2017). Peggy Hora was celebrating this breadth of endeavour in her reports prepared for the Adelaide 'Thinker In Residence' program more than a decade ago (Hora, 2010).

Research into crime prevention and reduction has shown that, with appropriate resourcing of preferred choices, not only can we turn around lives that have been drawn to crime, but we can also stem the flow of potential offenders into the justice system before they are caught by the criminal justice net (Homel, 2004; Homel & Freiberg, 2017; Homel & McGee, 2012; Homel et al., 2015).

Importantly, the research reveals that some choices are better than others. Indeed, it is not uncommon to find in the research that some crime prevention program adoptions have unintended consequences or counter-productive outcomes. Some programs and schemes work well for some crimes but not others; for some offenders but not for other offenders; in some cities and regions, but not in others. Some have worthwhile outcomes but only in the short term. The task for policymakers is to distil the research findings into workable options, fund the ones that have strongest outcomes, and pursue and prosecute them accordingly.

Over the last twenty-five years, the 'what works?' studies have been highly influential in such policymaking. While there have been valid criticisms of 'what works' approaches to crime prevention (see, for example, Cherney, 2000; Sutton, 2000, pp. 320–322), and while we know that nothing works *everywhere* (Laycock, 2014), one can safely say that the 'what works' quest has been, and continues to be, a laudable attempt to discern which programs should become the focus of policymakers' attention (and government and private spending) and which ones should not (for example, Bell & Coates, 2022; de Waard, 2022). A notable (and ground-breaking) example was the study undertaken at the University of Maryland throughout the 1990s (Sherman et al., 1997) designed to determine, using strict methodological criteria, the efficacy (read 'success') of crime prevention programs. The Campbell Collaboration, too, was set up to undertake similar tasks (Grabosky, 2012). Other examples of similar 'think-tanks' come quickly to mind. The Washington State Institute for Public Policy is a leading exponent of the art of determining the cost-effectiveness of specific initiatives (WSIPP, 2017). The Crime Reduction Toolkit (College of Policing, 2013) and EMMIE (an acronym for Effect, Mechanism, Moderators, Implementation and Economic cost) (Johnson et al., 2015) are two other examples of 'clearing house' repositories from which public and private researchers can view evaluations and thereby inform policymakers regarding the preferred options that emerge.

There is also an important distinction between 'what works?' in an evidence-based context, and 'what works?' in a meta-strategy context.

> With complex phenomena, it is best to follow not the most evidence-based strategy, but the best meta-strategy. The research question of which strategy works best is not as fertile as which meta-strategy works best. Rarely will the first strategy attempted work in a complex context that differs from the conditions of any controlled evaluation trial. A good meta-strategy informs stakeholders of results from the 'what works' literature and presumptively tries the most supported strategy first and then the second most supported strategy (after the first strategy fails). That presumption can be overridden in light of particular circumstances. Clinicians, by analogy,

try one therapy after another for a patient, informed by their knowledge of the outcomes of randomised controlled trials and their knowledge of particular cases, including what other medications patients are taking, their capabilities for surviving side effects, how strong their hearts are, and much more. (Braithwaite, 2022, pp. 441–442)

In other words, there will be a range of evaluative tools that can be utilised. Bringing them all together in a meta-analysis provides a rich vein of material for policymakers.

The importance of evaluations in this field cannot be over-stated. Clancey, Fisher, and Yeung remind us that the landscape has in the past been bleak, in that:

crime prevention continues to be a 'stop-and-start affair' and that its widespread adoption has progressed in the absence of evaluations necessary to provide evidence of its benefits in Australia ... (Clancey et al., 2016, p. 324)

Thirty years ago I gave some consideration to this issue. I explained the necessity of evaluation and the variety of options available to those who undertake evaluative tasks. I noted that most commentators in the business of evaluation are clear that there must be a middle ground between, on the one hand, no evaluation at all, and, on the other hand, evaluative research where its cost is disproportionate to its usefulness. I cited the opinion of academics who offer the guideline that between 5% and 10% of the overall cost of any project strategy should be devoted to its ongoing evaluation (Sarre, 1994, pp. 45–46).

The upshot of the evaluative quest is a remarkable wealth of knowledge. We are blessed with information. It is time that our policies and practices reflected that fact.

It's now time to consider how much crime there is, and where it is.

CHAPTER 2

Crime Trends

Abstract This chapter points to the fact that crime rates, especially property crime rates, have been trending downwards in all modern Western democracies since the mid-1990s. It points to Australian data that show that we are consistent with the international 'crime drop' trends. There are, however, some exceptions to the crime drop, notably (and tragically) violence against women and children, and the modern scourge of cybercrime. The chapter rejects the view that a key reason for this reduction is the high imprisonment rate that has stretched government budgets in recent years. In contrast, a Productivity Commission report provides sage advice regarding how governments might reduce prison numbers by focusing on strategies to keep Australians, especially First Nations peoples, out of prison. Finally, the chapter introduces the book published five decades ago by Norval Morris and Gordon Hawkins whose challenge to their readers in 1970 was a motivator for the writing of this book.

Keywords Crime rates · Property crime · Personal crime · Counter-productive effects · Social cohesion

There is good news on the crime front. Most crime, especially property crime, has been trending downwards in all modern Western democracies since before the start of the twenty-first century (Baker, 2013). Indeed, crime rates were identified as having declined significantly since the early to mid-1990s (Weatherburn et al., 2016) and the decline shows no signs of altering its path (Weatherburn & Rahman, 2021). In Australia, victimisation surveys (conducted nationally for the last three decades) confirm these trends. National rates for break-in, robbery, motor vehicle theft, theft from a motor vehicle, malicious property damage, and other theft have been steadily declining over the last two decades. The proportion of Australian households experiencing malicious property damage fell from roughly one in 10 in 2008–2009 to one in 20 in 2018–2019 (ABS, 2019a). The homicide rate (0.82 deaths per year per 100,000 population) is the lowest ever since records have been kept, down 55% in the last 30 years (Productivity Commission, 2021).

It should be noted, however, that there are some anomalies. While personal crimes (most notably assault) have been in general long-term decline for decades, the rates of threatened assault, robbery, and sexual assault—especially violence against women and children—all rose between 2017–2018 and 2018–2019 (ABS, 2019a). Sadly, rates of domestic and family violence remain stubbornly high. Indeed, the number of people reporting sexual assault continued to increase over the past five years. According to police figures, in 2022 the rate of victimisation in sexual crimes was 124 per 100,000 population. In contrast, in 2016 the rate was 95 per 100,000 (Productivity Commission, 2024a, Table 6A.16). On the rise also is cybercrime, both cyber-dependent and cyber-enabled crime (Brewer et al., 2019; Broadhurst, 2017; Goldsmith & Wall, 2022; Prenzler & Sarre, 2021; Sarre, 2022, 2023; Sarre & Prenzler, 2023; Voce & Morgan, 2023; Wortley & Prichard, 2023). It is difficult, if not impossible, to tackle cybercriminality with traditional law enforcement means because offenders can enter cyberspace from anywhere in the world. It remains a vexed problem for policymakers.

At the same time as there have been long-term reductions in key crimes, there has not been any decrease in the use of the traditional crime control measures offered by the formal justice system. Governments continue to hire more police, install more prison beds, put in place greater restrictions on bail and parole, and legislate for harsher sentences (Travers et al., 2020; Tubex et al., 2015) irrespective of the vast array of evidence emerging from the literature that points to the often counterproductive effect of these measures (Clear & Frost, 2014). One such effect is the dramatic rise in prison numbers in Australia over the last 40 years. Australia's imprisonment rate rose from 86 per 100,000 adult population in 1984 to 202 per 100,000 in 2023. Australia now has over 40,000 men and women in prison on an average night, with almost forty per cent of them in custody on remand awaiting trial (ABS, 2024). The annual throughput of persons into and out of the prison system is twice as many as the daily population figure. This malaise affects marginalised groups especially. A third of all prisoners identify as Indigenous notwithstanding that First Nations Australians are only three per cent of the population (ABS, 2024).

In October 2021 the Productivity Commission presented its findings after having undertaken an investigation into Australia's prison system (Productivity Commission, 2021). The Commission calculated that the 33% rise in incarceration rates in the preceding twenty years came primarily from 'tough on crime' government policies, and that this had cost taxpayers about AU$13.5 billion more than if the imprisonment rate had remained steady.

In his report, Productivity Commissioner Stephen King pointed to United Nations data that showed the growth in Australia's imprisonment rates since 2003 was third highest in the Organisation for Economic Cooperation and Development (OECD), exceeded only by Turkey and Colombia. Mirroring the information provided by the Australian Bureau of Statistics, Commissioner King revealed that the rate of offending (numbers of offenders proceeded against per 100,000 population) fell by 18% in the decade to 2020. Over the same period, the imprisonment rate had risen 25% (Productivity Commission, 2021).

Put simply, crime is down, but more and more people are being sent to prison.

One might be tempted to suggest that these two trends are causally connected. Is there any evidence that the former is the result of the latter?

The answer found in the literature is 'no.' Researchers in the United States (when this issue was first raised) came to this conclusion more than two decades ago. In September 2000 the Sentencing Project (USA) released the findings from its study of US criminal justice trends from 1991 to 1998. They revealed that the twenty States with the highest increases in incarceration rates averaged a 13% reduction in crime while the 30 States with lower trajectories of incarceration increases saw crime drop by 17%. Indeed, a study a decade later revealed that when three States (New York, New Jersey, and California) reduced their prison populations (by about 25%) their crime rates declined at a faster pace than the national average (Sentencing Project, 2014). Simply stated, crime rates and imprisonment rates are not causally linked (Center on Juvenile and Criminal Justice, 2019; Durlauf & Nagin, 2011).

There is other evidence, too, that helps us to resist any temptation to link current high imprisonment rates to lower crime rates. Two key reasons can be readily identified:

1. There have been crime drops in jurisdictions where the rate of imprisonment has remained stable or declined. Indeed, in Queensland during the period 2003–2012 the imprisonment rate fell at the same time as violent and property crime fell (ABS, 2019b). There are nations, such as Finland, that enjoy a very low crime rate (Finland 2020) and a very low imprisonment rate (Prison Studies, 2020).
2. There are many reasons that have been identified as important precipitators of the drop in crime that have little to do with punitive criminal justice responses and more to do with economic prosperity (Hällsten et al., 2013), good policing strategies including enhanced surveillance devices (Sarre et al., 2014), enhanced social institutions (Currie, 2008), better and cheaper household and business security options (Farrell, 2013), and demographics (in 1995 the last of the baby boomers turned 35, the age at which criminality, generally speaking, declines).

Moreover, while longer sentences may reduce the rates of some crimes (by virtue of their incapacitative effect), the size of the crime-reductive effect is subject to diminishing returns; that is, the expenditures on extra prison beds will eventually outweigh any savings brought about by reductions in crime (Vollaard, 2012). Other research evidence shows that longer prison sentences for non-violent offenders are no more effective than shorter sentences in reducing recidivism (Leymon et al., 2022). Moreover, sixty per cent of adult Australian prisoners in custody on June 30, 2023 had been in prison prior to that sentence (ABS, 2024) which knocks a dent into the idea that prison has a specific deterrent effect. One must conclude that formal criminal justice processes, necessary as they may be, are but a blunt instrument in the fight against crime (Tonry, 2011). The provision of police and prosecution services, courts, and corrections are necessary but insufficient to guarantee citizen safety.

More and more persuasive has become the argument, in crime prevention terms, that a safe community is one that is built on trust, equality of opportunity, the development of strong social capital, and positive, welcoming, and durable neighbourhoods (Putnam, 2001; Wickes et al., 2022; Wilkinson & Pickett, 2009). Elliott Currie (1998), too, concluded, a quarter of a century ago, that formal criminal justice processes need to take a back step in preventing crime and focus on developing 'society'. Most persuasive in Currie's eyes is the argument that a secure community is one that is built on social investments designed to build people's lives in constructive and humane ways, and that enhance social cohesion.

How is Australia currently doing on the social cohesion score? Not particularly well, according to James O'Donnell.

> The sense of social inclusion and justice in Australia increased strongly during the height of the COVID-19 pandemic. Probably reflecting a positive public response to government measures to protect health and financial wellbeing, in 2020 there was an increase in the proportion of people who believe there was adequate financial support for people on low incomes, and a decline in the proportion who believe the gap between those with high and low incomes is too large. However, social inclusion and justice has declined sharply since 2020. In 2022, social cohesion on this measure is lower than it was before the pandemic. This has been driven by a renewed growth in the number of people who are concerned with economic inequality in Australia. The proportion of people who strongly agree that the gap in incomes is too large has increased from 31 per cent in 2019 to 36 per cent in 2022, while the proportion who strongly agree that 'Australia is a land of economic opportunity where in the long run, hard work brings a better life' has declined from 19 per cent in 2019 to just 14 per cent in 2022. (O'Donnell, 2022, p. 7)

The malaise has also been highlighted in a report from the Australian Council of Social Services (Davidson et al., 2023). For the period 1999 to 2019, the average incomes of the highest 5% of the population grew faster (by 59% overall) than those of the middle 20% (41%) and lowest 20% (46%) during this period. The wealthiest 20% now hold average wealth (82% of the value of all investment property and 78% of all shares and financial investments) that is six times the wealth of the middle 20% and ninety times that of the lowest 20% (Davidson et al., 2023, p. 9).

In 1970, Norval Morris and Gordon Hawkins published a watershed study which they entitled *The Honest Politicians' Guide to Crime*

Control. In this book they offered '…a cure for crime—not a sudden potion nor a lightning panacea but rather a legislative and administrative regimen which would substantially reduce the impact of crime' (Morris & Hawkins, 1970, p. ix). In their analysis of justice processes in the United States they set out a range of crime control 'ukases' (decrees) having assessed them for their efficacy. In Chapter 1 they criticise the laws that criminalise public drunkenness, possession of drugs, gambling, vagrancy, abortion, homosexuality, and delinquency, asserting that this type of approach to crime control is counterproductive. They then move (Chapter 2) to what they consider to be improvements to the research agenda, controversially rejecting calculations of the 'cost' of crime and instead demanding that researchers focus on the costs of crime *control*. Their Chapter 3 is a mix of reform ideas including stronger gun control, greater attention to the prevention of drink driving, and the abolition of capital punishment. Chapter 4 looks at improvements to police recruitment and higher salaries, and proper attention to police academies, resourcing, communications, technologies, and home protection. Chapter 5 sets out the authors' agenda to reform the American bail system, its corrections policies and the processes of probation and parole. Chapter 6 is devoted to juvenile courts, and the need for diversionary activities for young offenders rather than formal processes. Chapter 7 is devoted to addressing the shortcomings in psychological and psychiatric services in justice administration. Chapter 8 looks at preferable ways to attack organised crime, and in Chapter 9 the authors address need for properly funded crime and justice research units.

Their text contains a cornucopia of ideas, some of which have come to pass in the United States (for example, increased funding for evidence-based policy development and technologies available to police), some of which have been partially addressed (for example, promoting diversionary paths for juvenile offenders), and others that have been more difficult to implement or have not been actioned universally (for example, the abolition of the death penalty across the country).

The issues that they raise and the evidence that they examine is a little dated today. Indeed, they have an American focus, and not all of their conclusions were aimed at crime reduction (the abolition of capital punishment is one such matter). But the important lesson from their analysis for my purposes (and one that is not dated) is that the formal processes of justice (apprehension, prosecution, sentencing, and corrections) are not the panacea for the reduction of crime that many voters may think they are. Indeed, formal justice processes can often make the crime problem more acute.

I will return to their conclusions later in the book.

It is time to look at the role that police play in crime prevention.

CHAPTER 3

Policing and Crime Prevention

Abstract This chapter looks at the role that police play in crime prevention. It explains the distinction between 'reactive' policing and 'proactive' policing and explores why, despite the public's view that police action is fundamental to crime control, police are not a key reason for crime rates going up or down. Crime is, for the most part, outside of the control of the police. The chapter explains how police effectiveness is only as good as the general community's willingness to accept it, and reviews 'legitimacy' theory in this explanation. It describes the conflicting pressures on senior police managers to solve crime and disorder problems over which they have little control. It highlights the dilemma for uniformed police on patrol who are trying to satisfy the needs of communities that have multiple and often competing voices. Finally, it looks at the sometimes fractured relationships between police and First Nations Australians in the crime-reductive task.

Keywords Reactive policing · Proactive policing · Crime control · Police performance · Police culture

Police play a vital role in the justice landscape in Australia. Policing in Australia typically accounts for approximately two thirds of all Commonwealth and State justice-related expenditures (Productivity Commission,

2024a). Pleasingly, Australian police consistently enjoy a good public profile. Almost 74% of respondents report satisfaction with services provided by police (Productivity Commission, 2024a, Table 6A.6). There are minor variations across the eight State and Territory jurisdictions, but commentators agree that, generally speaking, police in Australia consistently deliver what has come to be expected of them, including responding to calls for assistance (referred to as 'reactive' policing), and in deterring criminal behaviour using a range of prophylactic measures (referred to as 'proactive' policing). This has been the case for at least three decades (Prenzler & Sarre, 2002; Sarre, 2004).

There have long been allegations, however, that police tend to focus on 'reactive' policing over 'proactive' policing because it is more immediate and more visible and thus satisfies the public perception of what 'real' policing is all about (Bayley, 1993; Sarre, 2003).

But there is abundant evidence that no matter what the reactive strategy, there is little discernible change in crime rates on that score alone (Sarre, 1997). Research from four decades ago told us that quicker response times and reliance upon reactive crime control expertise do not bring the rewards (lower crime rates and greater 'clear-up' rates) that are sought (Klockars, 1981, pp. 160–166). Indeed, evaluations of police performance in the United States have shown that increasing visible police presence in marked police cars did not appear to have any effect on crime rates, nor in reducing fear (Bayley, 1994, p. 125). Increasingly it has become apparent that solving crime is poorly related to the number of police assigned to the criminal investigation task.

Why might this be the case? Crime is, for the most part, outside of the control of the police. Crime trends across all societies appear to move up and down regardless of the financial commitment of governments to support police demands, and to supply the hardware and personnel resources they say they need. Experts have long acknowledged that simply injecting more resources into law enforcement has only a small effect upon crime rates.

> Ninety percent of the variation in crime rates among population aggregations of substantial size can be predicted by population density, ethnic heterogeneity, unemployment, income, school-leaving and single households-headed-by-women. How then can the police, whose activities are only part of criminal justice processing, be expected to make a measurable impact on crime? (Bayley, 1993, p. 3)

There have been marked improvements in policing since that opinion was offered. The advent of what became known as 'intelligence-led' police and the consequential 'hot spot' strategies (Ratcliffe, 2008) have been able to replace, with some success, random patrolling, and isolated investigative practices. Moreover, there is growing evidence that police are more likely today to recognise that there are great benefits in linking their work to the work of health professionals and liaising with them (Bartkowiak-Théron & Asquith, 2016). But it is widely accepted by police theorists such as David Dixon (2005) that police have no direct effect on what are consistently identified as the root causes of much offending such as intergenerational trauma, poor urban conditions, mental illness, homelessness, child maltreatment and abuse, socially disengaged individuals, ill-conceived discriminatory laws, and failed economies. Simply stated, the legal and physical powers of police have only a small (if any) effect upon the economic and political milieu in which we live. It is simply not possible for police alone to forestall all the precursors to crime.

Similarly, police effectiveness is only as good as the general community's willingness to accept it, a field of research referred to as 'legitimacy' theory (Barkworth & Murphy, 2015; Hough et al., 2013; Mazerolle et al., 2015; Murphy & Barkworth, 2014; Sargeant et al., 2012; Tyler & Fagan, 2008). According to this theory, crime reduction is assisted by police placing an emphasis on procedural justice. The evidence shows that procedural justice is important for influencing citizens' emotional reactions to the police and compliance with the law. By engaging with the public in a polite, respectful, and empathetic manner, police officers can reduce negative sentiments and emotions directed at them, thereby increasing people's willingness to comply with police directions, both immediately and in the future, and supply them with information. In other words, it is the style and manner of police-citizen interactions that give rise to effective policing.

Commendably, Australian police take very seriously their role in crime prevention. They are genuine in their desire to elevate 'proactive' policing as a principal goal. This is borne out by the emphasis given to 'problem-oriented' policing ('POP') in recent years, although it was first mooted more than four decades ago (Goldstein, 1979). POP is designed to prevent the recurrence of problem behaviours which fall within the remit of police by identifying problem spots using SARA, that is, scanning, analysis, response, and assessment (Bullock & Tilley, 2009). There are significant references under the rubric 'crime prevention' in the various annual reports published by police services around the country. For example, SAPOL refers readers to its report against the objective: 'a prevention first approach to reduce community impact of offending, support victims and provide effective criminal justice services' (SAPOL, 2021).

However, Carriere and Ericson (1989) asserted that police find it difficult to position themselves as crime preventers rather than crime fighters. Writing about Canadian police, they were of the view that the lip-service paid to crime prevention by police has less to do with reducing criminal damage and criminality generally and more to do with providing a political agenda that would guarantee them enhanced powers of investigation, arrest, questioning of suspects and firepower (Carriere & Ericson, 1989, pp. 96–97).

In Australia, too, there is a suspicion that police consultation on proactive crime prevention takes place only with those with a vested interest in the prevailing social order. That being the case, the information flowing to the police is skewed in favour of those who stand to gain most from police involvement. There are thus conflicting pressures on police to solve crime and disorder problems. It is not uncommon, too, for police to find that they are being pulled in opposite directions in order to satisfy divergent interests.

> For example, police may be asked by influential members of the community to implement a policy (for example, a night curfew affecting young people) that acts counter to the aims of local crime prevention strategists appealing to young people to become involved with and trusted by their community's civic leaders. (Sarre, 2000, p. 75)

Little may have changed in the thirty years since Peter Grabosky offered the same view:

> In a homogeneous society, mutual penetration of police and citizenry may be in the public interest. But in a heterogeneous or otherwise divided society, those interests which are generally dominant may also be expected to dominate citizen participation in law enforcement. Unequal participation need not lead inevitably to unequal justice, but the potential shortcomings of participatory imbalance are such that certain checks or compensatory devices may be required ... Private citizens are not always motivated by a sense of public service or civic virtue. (Grabosky, 1992, p. 266)

Those who have no 'voice' have little incentive to consult with police. Indeed, what is the 'community'? Social groups and networks are not geographical anymore. It is likely that communities will have a dozen or more voices.

Moreover, the various priorities, agendas and aims of these agencies can sometimes cut across or undermine each other's work. Curfews of young people provide an example. Police use curfews in order to keep stray lads off the streets. A young lad who otherwise is simply 'trying the system on' breaks the curfew and is arrested. His life in the justice system begins, all because he was being provocative. The crime prevention workers at the local level who were hoping to keep him away from the justice system by offering a recreation club or other adventure group have cause to wring their hands. The point is that not all people concerned to bring about crime prevention are singing from the same song book.

It is timely to review the shameful over-representation of First Nations people in the criminal justice system and much of that malaise has been brought about by police methods and attitudes. Two centuries ago, caught up in a world of frontier warfare, attack, and reprisal, colonial police, even those who may have harboured some sympathy for native populations, had little option but to carry out their often-retributive tasks. The upshot of this situation is clear:

> For many Aboriginal people the first contact they had with the police was with a paramilitary force of dispossession, dispensing summary justice and on some occasions involved in the indiscriminate massacre of clan and tribal groups. (Cunneen, 2001, p. 50)

But the modern breakdown in relationships is not simply an historical legacy. Ongoing suspicion and mutual antagonism has been fuelled by the contemporary experience of Aboriginal Australians with police as well. The late Elliott Johnston QC, one of the writers of the final report of the Royal Commission into Aboriginal Deaths in Custody in 1991, commented as follows:

> [F]ar too much police intervention in the lives of Aboriginal people ... has been arbitrary, discriminatory, racist and violent. There is absolutely no doubt in my mind that the antipathy which so many Aboriginal people have

towards police is based not just on historical contact but upon the contemporary experience of contact with many police officers. (Royal Commission, 1991, p. 195)

Even today, offending behaviour in First Nations communities is inextricably linked to, and enmeshed with, victimisation, substance abuse, and poverty (Weatherburn & Ramsey, 2016). Other commentators have been critical of the ambiguities and cultural contradictions associated with 'negotiated' justice, where non-Indigenous interests remain paramount (Broadhurst, 2002, p. 277; Putt & Sarre, 2018; Taylor et al., 2021). Police today, even with the best intentions, find bridge-building into First Nations communities a difficult task.

Furthermore, status and promotion within the police ranks is still strongly linked to successes in crime fighting, not in crime prevention. Police culture regularly undervalues skills in crime prevention, excellence in community relations and victim support (Carriere & Ericson, 1989). So, while lip-service is paid to the prophylactic role of police in the face of crime, it is unlikely to be embraced fully by the rank-and-file officer.

Put simply, police services are necessary but not sufficient in the crime prevention task. In the next chapter we read how they have been assisted by a useful and available set of allies.

CHAPTER 4

Public/Private Partnerships in Crime Prevention

Abstract This chapter explains how a great deal of the responsibility for policing has shifted away from governments (the public police) to the private sector, typically through private security companies who are available under contract for governments and private businesses alike. Indeed, on some estimates there are twice as many full time and part time operatives who put on a security uniform each week in Australia than there are police officers. That being the case, their role in crime prevention is not only useful but essential. The chapter explores the factors that have given impetus to this national and international growth, and the relationships between private operatives and public police, especially by virtue of the former providing the latter with computer hardware and software in the fight against counterterrorism, cybercrime, and organised crime. The chapter ends by weighing up the pros and cons of an expansion of this vast empire of crime-reductive agents.

Keywords Private security · Regulation · Cybercriminality · Mixed economy of policing · Pluralisation of policing

Optimal crime prevention effectiveness cannot be achieved by State, Territory, and Federal police alone. The 'policing' task needs greater resources. In order to respond to the demand, a great deal of the responsibility for policing has shifted away from governments to the private sector (Button, 2008; Sarre & Prenzler, 2018, 2021a, 2021b). Indeed, Philip Stenning asserts that the 'police', as commonly thought of, are now but one member of an ever extended 'policing family' (Stenning, 2009, p. 23). This regulatory phenomenon has been expanding for at least four decades (Grabosky, 1995; van Steden & Sarre, 2010). A keen observer of the field, and an early researcher in the area, Clifford Shearing, made the following observation in 1989:

> I began to notice that there were a lot of people around who behaved like public police in all sorts of ways and responded to many of the same troubles but did not wear signs announcing themselves as POLICE and were not part of 'the criminal justice system'... I looked at these 'private security' people. One of the first things I discovered was that not only were they not part of the criminal justice system but very often they had nothing whatsoever to do with it .... (Shearing, 1989, p. 174)

There are a number of key factors that have given considerable impetus to this growth. These include greater demand from consumers for effective local security in their neighbourhoods, an increasing cost differential between private security options and police, vast improvements in the ability of security services to provide inexpensive technological solutions to security problems, and the internationalisation of crime, especially cybercrime.

In recent years, there has been a marked development of, and expansion in, ties between police and private security, and a considerable improvement in these relationships (Prenzler & Sarre, 2021, 2022). The private security sector itself has been keen to expand its markets and establish its credibility with public agencies. Significantly, calls for cooperation have come from governments too, seeking cost savings, especially in relation to the sorts of tasks that do not necessarily need specialist policing services, such as guarding, monitoring CCTV, issuing fines, and checking bags at entrances to public and private precincts.

The most common form of engagement of the private sector by Australian governments in policing has been through the development of formal public–private partnerships (Sarre & Prenzler, 2000). Other engagements include private agents working with state and regulatory authorities, both with community groups (government funded and privately funded), and with non-public third parties in a variety of crime control roles, referred to as 'third-party' policing (Ransley & Mazerolle, 2017).

It is thus not uncommon to find state governments hiring and deploying private transit officers, and local government councils hiring private personnel to maintain a security presence in parks and at beach fronts. CCTV installations, monitored chiefly by private personnel, are now ubiquitous in public spaces under the auspices of local and state governments. At the national level, too, the counter-terrorism agenda has allowed private security operators to exhibit their skills and deploy their hardware in an anti-terrorism environment (Sarre, 2012a). Thus, the state, through its purchasing power to supplement its police services, is a key driver of this mixed economy of policing.

On the one hand, this trend towards public and private cooperation is a good thing: the private sector is well-resourced and ready to participate in this exercise of supplementation (Sarre & Prenzler, 2017). Moreover, the private sector's prophylactic measures (such as multi-factor authentication of internet users capable of thwarting cybercrime) have been embraced enthusiastically by governments, too, because only the private sector has the financial resources at the ready to develop such tools.

On the other hand, the private sector can be self-serving and has been accused of being more beholden to the protection of its shareholders' interests than to the common weal, and risking the civil liberties enjoyed by citizens in a democracy (Prenzler & Sarre, 2014b). Policing partnerships can give rise to non-police 'eyes' having access to confidential data, too. Different rules, protocols, and procedures may apply to relevant agents, depending upon who their paymasters are (Chang et al., 2018, pp. 108–110). Moreover, if there are inadequate licensing systems, poor training and insufficient supervision of private operatives, public/private partnerships may quickly break down. Private interests may be less inclined to watch for any bias that may be exhibited in their operations. For example, the Australian Human Rights Commission noted a racial bias emerging in the implementation of facial recognition technology developed by the private sector, and called, in October 2021, for a moratorium on its use without a stronger regulatory framework being put in place (Australian Human Rights Commission, 2021). Moreover, the legal rights, responsibilities, and immunities that these partnerships toss up are, for the most part, uncertain (Sarre, 2008, 2014).

That having been said, the private operator plays a crucial role in the policing landscape.

It is useful to give an illustration of the importance of private security initiatives when it comes to crime prevention in relation both to property crime and crimes against the person. In 2013, a ground-breaking study was published by Graham Farrell (Farrell, 2013) in which he examined fifteen reasons (hypotheses) that had been offered by various commentators to explain the significant drop in crime, especially violent crime, across the Western world since the mid-1990s. The hypotheses were as follows: general economic prosperity, capital punishment, more guns in private hands, (and the converse) fewer guns in private hands, prison numbers (more people behind bars means fewer crimes can be committed), police numbers (more police eyes can observe more crime), targeted police strategies, legalised abortion, programs for inter-ethnic harmony, consumer confidence, lower drug availability, the removal of lead from gasoline, demographics, the emergence of institutions designed to strengthen social capital, and better and more affordable electronic security systems for both homes and businesses.

Farrell then subjected these hypotheses to a series of tests which he devised. He examined the empirical evidence; the cross-national stability of the data; any pre-existing trends in the data; the power of the data to explain criminality that was *not* decreasing; and the nominated reason's perceived effectiveness across different crimes. He concluded that the only hypothesis that satisfied all of the tests was the last one: better and more affordable electronic security systems (see also Farrell et al., 2014). On this thesis, a significant proportion of the responsibility for crime reduction is firmly in the hands of technically proficient private sector operatives.

While the Farrell conclusion is based upon only one analysis, and will attract some detractors, including myself, by the way its findings degrade the importance of long-term social justice initiatives in the crime prevention arsenal, his study is mentioned here because it re-states the important role of the private sector. Certainly, a citizen, when moving around the community in daily life today, is far more likely to be directed, challenged, or searched by a private security officer than by a police officer.

International research, too, has found that privately funded security operations directly contribute to significant reductions in criminal victimisation (van Dijk, 2008, pp. 129ff). Moreover, the fight against the growing scourge of cybercrime has been, and continues to be, a site of strong cooperation between national police and the private sector (Gill, 2013).

The private policing field is characterised the world over by a heterogeneous composition of companies that offer capital-intensive and labour-intensive services. This has had major consequences for the way in which society perceives the 'policing' task. On any reading of history and of the trends, state police cannot be the sole guarantors of order now or in the future. Even if it were physically possible, it is simply not economically feasible.

CHAPTER 5

Preventing White-Collar Crime

Abstract This chapter explores the prevention of crime that is typically committed by people who have money and power. It provides yet another example of where the best crime prevention strategies may be found outside of the criminal justice system. While some corporate crime can be identified as flowing from a rational, cost-benefit analysis, there is, on the evidence, little deterrence in a criminal law response to aberrant white-collar behaviour. This is often because of the existence of a corporate culture that is impervious to such legal threats. Moreover, the harm has already been done when the criminal justice system (and the criminal laws it relies upon) is called upon to intervene. The chapter explores the idea that addressing and shaping the culture of organisations may provide a better option for regulatory control. Finally, the chapter provides suggestions about how best to encourage corporate and business attitudes, behaviours, and incentives such that criminal conduct is less likely to occur.

Keywords Occupational crime · Corporate crime · Workplace violence · Criminal negligence · Deterrence

In 1949, the noted sociologist Edwin Sutherland published his watershed book *White-Collar Crime* (Sutherland, 1949/1983). In his work, he developed the idea that criminologists ought to be focusing more of their attention upon the types of crimes committed by people of respectability and social status in the course of their occupation rather than those who typically fell into crime from a low socio-economic milieu. There has been much disagreement since that time about what constitutes or should constitute white-collar crime, and, indeed, there is, to this day, conjecture about how far its boundaries extend. One can safely argue, however, that the phenomenon extends not only to what might be referred to as *occupational* crime (crimes committed by persons in the course of their work), but also to *corporate* crime (crimes committed by the organisations themselves using organisational resources). And it is into this latter category that one can place two types of crime. The first is corporate behaviour that one might safely categorise as criminal, such as trading while insolvent or deceptively charging for services that were never intended to be delivered. The second is corporate violence or violations of rights, such as causing death in a workplace or making decisions in the workplace that have the effect of allowing a death to occur (Gobert & Punch, 2003) or engaging in environmental damage, poisoning or destruction (White & Monod, 2017).

While some corporate misbehaviour can be identified as flowing from a rational choice, a crime-reductive response that relies principally upon general deterrence is unrealistic (Tomasic, 2005; Thornton et al., 2005). This is because of the existence of a corporate culture that may be impervious to such legal threats. Governments are, however, typically drawn to deterrence theory despite the lack of evidence regarding its effectiveness, often drawing attention to the 'one bad apple' (the aberrant loner) as the cause of white-collar crime. (One might speculate that this narrative avoids drawing attention to the alternative narrative, namely that the government is to blame for its own inaction on social and economic fronts. No government is going to find that explanation politically acceptable, so it is rare if ever proffered.)

Moreover, when it comes to penalising that 'bad apple' (a specific deterrence approach) there is, principally, reliance by governments (keen to be seen as 'doing something' about white-collar crime) on championing the *threat* of punishment as its main crime prevention tool. But there are weaknesses in that approach. For a start, few corporate executives have a criminal record, and, by contrast, many can boast a distinguished history of public and community service, so the likelihood of a court giving a prison sentence to them is low. Thus, whatever deterrent effect there may be is soon diluted.

There is quantitative evidence, too, of the limited deterrent effect of the threat of a custodial sentence. Durlauf and Nagin (2011) point out that variation in sentence severity—within levels that are plausible in Western societies—does not appear to have much, if any, impact on crime. Nor does a period of imprisonment appear to decrease subsequent offending in this country (Sarre, 2012b; Weatherburn, 2010). Almond, from his research in the United Kingdom, contends that the public is often more concerned with controlling the underlying risks of corporate malfeasance (in his focus, corporate manslaughter) than the vilification of offenders through imprisonment (Almond, 2008, p. 464).

In recent years there has emerged the idea that addressing the culture of the organisation (a culture that allows white-collar crime to grow and fester) might be a better crime prevention option than relying upon the *ex post facto* response of the criminal law. This has become relevant more recently with the release of the Australian Human Rights Commission's Independent Review into Commonwealth Parliamentary Workplaces (Australian Human Rights Commission, 2022). One might argue that the community now has higher expectations about what that culture might look like, particularly when it comes to matters such as gender equality, workplace respect, and public accountability for workplace behaviour more generally (Livings & Sarre, 2023).

Let me explain how this might work. Traditionally, the imposition of corporate criminal liability falls under the common law doctrine of 'identification.' Under this (and its stablemate the 'attributional' approach), corporate culpability derives from the actions of an identified individual whose criminality can be attributable to that of the corporation, either because the individual was influential enough within the corporation to serve as its 'controlling mind' or because the individual was acting at the behest of the company as an agent or officer (Sarre & Richards, 2005).

While this sounds good, this approach has problems insofar as it does not reflect, or cater to, the fragmented decision-making and responsibilities of those involved in carrying out the actions of corporate entities. As Gobert and Punch explain:

> [The] criminal law was not developed with companies in mind. Concepts such as *mens rea* [the guilty mind] and *actus reus* [the behaviour identified as misconduct], which make perfectly good sense when applied to

individuals, do not translate easily to an inanimate fictional entity such as a corporation. Trying to apply these concepts to companies is a bit like trying to squeeze a square peg into a round hole. (Gobert & Punch, 2003, p. 10)

It has been suggested that a more productive way of preventing white-collar crime is to address the corporate culture within an organisation. This notion explores whether there is a way that shaping corporate culture and working with it (a managerial approach) rather than fighting against it (a legislative approach with criminal sanctions attached) can better prevent the possibility of corporate wrongdoing. For example, while a corporation may outwardly claim to be concerned with occupational health and safety, if the pressure on individual managers is to meet financial or time pressures, then there may be a temptation for corners to be cut. Worker safety is thus compromised; financial transgressions become more likely (Livings & Sarre, 2023).

It is useful to look at how 'cultural' responses, added to the regulatory toolbox, might better prevent white-collar crime. Let me illustrate how that might apply in the context of industrial manslaughter.

In the case of *The Queen v Leighton Contractors Pty Ltd* (Unreported, County Court of Victoria, per Judge Gebhardt, 27 May 2004) a construction company (Leighton) had been convicted of serious breaches of the Victorian Occupational Health and Safety Act. Leighton had subcontracted with Sergi Services Pty Ltd to provide crane services for the construction of a bridge. On 8 October 2000, one of the concrete beams used in the construction collapsed, killing Mr Sergi and injuring a number of his co-workers. Leighton was charged with failing to provide and maintain plant that was safe and without risk to health. The company pleaded guilty.

Judge Gebhardt found evidence of gross shoddiness and an indifference to a standard of engineering and construction precision which was required in that kind of work. He ordered that the company pay fines, plus large payouts to two charities and a further sum into the trust funds of the deceased worker's children (Catanzariti, 2004).

For the first time in legal history in Australia, an order was then made that the directors meet with Victorian WorkSafe representatives three times a year, and to report these meetings in the company's annual reports. The company was also ordered to assist in the implementation of a new industry standard for bridge beam construction by paying more than $40,000 to the development of a training program for construction workers. Furthermore, the company agreed to approach two Melbourne universities for the purpose of improving occupational health and safety training for engineers associated with the design of temporary structures for bridge construction.

This is a legal sanctions approach (albeit wrapped in the necessary criminal law 'blanket') that goes to the heart of what a 'culture' approach might look like. The training and the new industry standards implementation are designed to reduce the possibility of harm up front, rather than rely upon a criminal law response after the damage has been done.

Whether 'culture' can be tied successfully to the criminal law to establish corporate criminal responsibility is a matter of some conjecture (Tomasic, 2017, p. 221). Discussion to date has been hampered by the multi-layered complexities and political tensions involved in drafting laws designed to bring responsible persons to account while remaining faithful to basic precepts of criminal responsibility and punishment policy. Ben Livings and I take a far more sanguine view, figuring that authorities should test the waters with targeted and strategic prosecutions that explore the effectiveness of a 'culture' approach to culpability in those jurisdictions where that legislative possibility exists, such as in the Australian Capital Territory (Livings & Sarre, 2023; Sarre & Richards, 2005).

Commentators have suggested that there is broad deterrent power in other options, too, such as divestment of company equity, adverse publicity, corporate probation (with remedial and rehabilitative conditions), disqualifications from certain commercial activities, receiverships (or ordering someone else to run the company), the threat of the loss of limited liability and ultimately a company's winding-up (Clough, 2005, pp. 120–130). These options reinforce the value of a multi-faceted approach to sentencing corporations in the event of culpable behaviour, be it financial fraud that leaves victims impecunious, or dangerous behaviour that leads to injury or death in the workplace (Sarre, 2019a).

In sum: to counter white-collar crime, there needs to be embedded within corporate entities themselves and their professional communities a variety of social control mechanisms including a recognition that development of a good corporate culture will provide a safer and less financially vulnerable environment for all. Simply stated, reliance upon a justice system 'deterrence' model has not been effective to date. The status quo that relies upon enforcement of the criminal law and deterrent penalties has proven to be largely ineffective. This model can well be described as 'too little, too late.'

The trick here is to find out how best to encourage such attitudes, behaviours, and incentives with or without the threat of serious legal sanction. Professional communities should be rewarding companies that display exemplary corporate governance behaviour (Hill, 2002). I argue that the development of good corporate culture is far more likely to be an effective regulatory tool than persisting with an *ex post facto*, mostly ineffective, and often unfair means of tackling corporate malfeasance.

CHAPTER 6

Surveillance as a Crime Prevention Tool

Abstract This chapter explores the way that the monitoring of persons and information can and does assist crime prevention, either in terms of its deterrent effect or the way that matters can be prosecuted on the strength of the evidence gleaned from digital and other electronic surveillance devices. It explores the mixed blessing of surveillance, weighing the spectre of the omnipresent prying 'eyes' of the digital world against the value that that world has had in tracking, monitoring, and convicting those who would commit crime, including internationally based cyber-criminals. There is little doubt that, despite the fact that this level of tracking would have been used by the secret police of yesteryear and feared by citizens, it has become commonplace and accepted, if not welcomed today. The chapter explains in detail the phenomenon of cybercrime, and possible avenues towards its control. It concludes with an observation about the important role of the Office of Australian Information Commissioner.

Keywords Electronic surveillance · Digital world · CCTV · Privacy · Cybercrime

Surveillance is the ability to monitor, observe, and record what, where, and when something happens. It involves the monitoring of any person, place, or object to obtain information. Of great interest today is the rapid growth in technological innovations that make surveillance more accessible, and more covert. These advances in technology have largely legitimated surveillance as a multi-purpose policing 'tool' that is not only available to police and regulatory agencies but also to private individuals and organisations.

Daily, vast numbers of citizens around the world are being observed through the surveillance activities of others. Police, intelligence agencies, corporations, employers, media, and property owners, many by using their privately contracted security personnel and service providers, are all now capable of observing, monitoring, and filming the activities of others, including listening in on their conversations. They are accessing their data, too, for marketing purposes at the lower end of the scale and for intelligence analysis at the higher end (Andrejevic, 2012). 'On-selling' of electronic information and the sorting of consumer databases are a regular part of global commerce (Dearne, 2001).

Electronic surveillance has played an important role in reducing criminal offending generally. It has inextricably linked the public and private sectors associated with it. The most pervasive of electronic surveillance is the visual imaging provided by the digital camera, linked to a CCTV system. These cameras are now widespread throughout the world (Gill, 2006). CCTV can accommodate overt and covert cameras, traffic flow cameras, speed infringement cameras, and red-light intersection cameras. Casinos, department stores, convenience and fuel shops, streets and car parks, reserves and nature parks, railway and bus stations, universities, and sports arenas are all likely candidates for CCTV surveillance. These cameras can be and have been deployed by national, regional, and local governments in 'public' areas and by the private sector on and around private property. The vast majority are operated and monitored by private security personnel to whom such responsibilities have been outsourced by contractual arrangements.

There has been some academic interest in the potential for abuse of CCTV, principally by virtue of the public intrusiveness exercised by those who operate and monitor the cameras and the potential misuse of the images collected and stored by CCTV hardware (Prenzler & Sarre, 2017). In days gone by this was not a problem; access to recorded video was relatively easy to monitor and thus control due to the inherent technical limitations found in CCTV systems. However, these technical limitations no longer apply (Gill, 2006). YouTube, Vimeo, Instagram, Twitter, Tik

Tok, Facebook, and other social media platforms now provide mechanisms for the immediate worldwide distribution of recorded video and images. These advances bring with them opportunities to use images and digital data in innovative ways to manage and respond effectively to crises and crime risks, but they also raise privacy concerns. An Australian casino in 2011, for example, was exposed as an employer that allowed its security staff to collect and copy CCTV footage of patrons and other staff for their own prurient interests and in clear defiance of privacy courtesies, if not privacy rights (Gill, 2006, p. 456). New, stringent company policies have been more recently reviewed in the New Zealand context (Blumenfeld et al., 2020).

Pleasingly, the debate over privacy vis-à-vis the ubiquity of surveillance has long been a site of policy unease (for example, Fasman, 2021; Millard, 2012). Much of the task of crime prevention today has less to do with traditional police methods (in the criminal justice tradition) and more to do with equipment and interactions related to surveillance.

Is this a matter that should give us concern?

Let me observe that previous generations have always feared external scrutiny; the Orwellian 'Big Brother' was the governmental overseer to be avoided, indeed, rebuked. Fast forward to the twenty-first century, and every move of a mobile phone user is tracked by one's non-government communications provider. The Global Positioning System (GPS) chip in our cars sends information back to the map installer. Our credit card transactions are recorded and stored by private companies. The 'QR' (quick response) code check-ins that were regularly used in the fight against the global pandemic allowed others to know our exact location and interests (Ruoti, 2022). Peter Grabosky reminds us of the surveillance consequences of the electronic age, exacerbated by the response of governments around the globe to the pandemic:

> [D]igital technology has enabled surveillance to a degree that is positively Orwellian. Proposals for the real-time tracing of individuals' physical location and their proximity to infected persons might appeal to some idealists, but the same application would have been welcomed by the secret police of yesteryear, and indeed, those of today. (Grabosky, 2023, p. viii)

Are our lives safer and less prone to victimisation by virtue of these tools? One can but speculate. Moreover, it is difficult to calculate whether the costs of privacy loss and expenditures associated with monitoring are worth whatever benefits may accrue.

Let me examine that conundrum in the context of the growing phenomenon of worldwide cybercrime.

Cybercrime has been variously referred to as 'computer crime', 'computer-related crime', 'hi-tech crime', 'technology-enabled crime', 'e-crime', or 'cyberspace crime'. Grabosky (2007) helpfully classified three general forms, including crimes where the computer is used as the instrument of crime, crimes where the computer is incidental to the offence, and crimes where the computer is the target of crime. McGuire and Dowling (2013) developed a similar idea, classifying cybercrime into 'cyber-enabled' crime and 'cyber-dependent' crime. Cyber-enabled crimes are traditional crimes facilitated by the deployment of computers. Cyber-dependent crimes are those crimes that would not exist without the technology. Another useful classification is the one devised by Gordon and Ford (2006) who divided activities into Type I and Type II offences. Type I cybercrimes are crimes which are more technical in nature (for example, hacking). Type II cybercrime is a crime that relies on human contact rather than technology (for example, illegal online gambling).

Regardless of how cybercrime is classified, there is little doubt that its range is broad—it includes fraudulent financial transactions, identity theft, romance scams, theft of electronic information for commercial gain, drug-trafficking, money-laundering, aberrant voyeuristic activities, image-based sexual abuse, harassment, stalking and other threatening behaviours (Bailey et al., 2021; Sarre et al., 2018; Teunissen et al., 2022). While these sorts of activities have always been classified as criminal, they are now so much easier to pursue with a computer and a modem, and from anywhere in the world.

Cybercrime includes terrorist recruitment, and terrorist financing. It includes implementing malware attacks designed to disrupt a business by destroying its database. It includes the activities of the 'hacktivist', someone who protests an organisation's actions or policies by orchestrating a denial of service (Sarre et al., 2018). Today's criminals can commit cybercrime without the need for high-level technical skills. In fact, the internet can, itself, assist, with 'do-it-yourself' malware kits available in online forums.

A threat report in 2017 by the Australian Cyber Security Centre notes that 'malicious cyber activity against Australia's national and economic interests is increasing in frequency, scale, sophistication and severity'

(Australian Cyber Security Centre, 2017, p. 16). Cybercrime is thus an escalating problem for national and international police and security agencies.

A preferred prevention path through this dilemma is available. It must start with putting appropriate rules in place. These rules need to ensure that we can enjoy the benefits of the digital age without bringing us closer to a surveillance society in which our every move is monitored, tracked, recorded, and scrutinised by governments and private interests.

However, one new rule, to my mind, has little substance and a potential for counter-productivity. New laws came into effect in 2015 in Australia that demand that all telecommunications providers keep their metadata (information about the calls on their lines) for two years so that the data can be tracked and collated. Metadata retention relies heavily upon the cooperation of the private sector (Australian Parliament, 2017). In order to frustrate and block those who would orchestrate organised crime, or who would perpetrate violence in the name of some particular ideology, governments now have the capacity to keep track of metadata by enlisting the compliance of private telecommunications companies (Kowalick et al., 2018). It is a scheme that has been given the green light to continue for the foreseeable future so long as more transparency regarding its effectiveness is mandated (Australian Government, 2023a; Sarre & Prenzler, 2023). Its effectiveness is, however, impossible to gauge. Its cost is in the hundreds of millions of dollars.

What controls should society employ over the private sector to monitor its engagement in cyber surveillance? What degree of intrusion is acceptable? There are no easy answers, especially given that modern society appears uncertain about what levels of privacy its citizens demand, and the extent to which its citizens trust private operators to manage their clients' private data.

On the one hand, there is the view that we should regulate strictly the storage and use of consumers' personal data (not just metadata) held by private companies, given that digital data can spread worldwide in a matter of seconds, or can be hacked, or can be used to target our preferences. On this view, we should be very cautious of any surveillance that allows an emboldening of private agencies to spy upon the legitimate activities of those whom they (or any other authorities) deem 'undesirable'.

On the other hand, there is a strong sense that citizens' lives can be enhanced by having a ready supply of data available to anyone who wishes to access it. The new generations of digital users appear to be ambivalent about how much privacy they are willing to sacrifice in the rush to maintain contemporaneous contact with the world.

The recent Australian experience on this front helps us through this choice. On May 8, 2017, the Australian Government tabled the Productivity Commission's *Data Availability and Use Inquiry* (Productivity Commission, 2018). The Inquiry made 41 recommendations designed to shift from policies based on risk avoidance towards policies based on value, choice, transparency, and confidence in the digital world. A year later, on May 1, 2018, the government committed to establishing the National Data Commissioner office, introducing legislation to improve the sharing, use and reuse of public sector data while maintaining the strong security and privacy protections the community expects, and introducing a Consumer Data Right to allow consumers of data to share their usage with private service competitors and comparison services. The government has enshrined in legislation that data sharing and release is only authorised for specified purposes (such as informing and assessing government policy and research and development with public benefits), and only if data safeguards are met (Flannery, 2019). Today the Office of Australian Information Commissioner covers this field. Its role is to monitor breaches of privacy. It provides an important safeguard against abuse. The Commissioner plays a crucial role in regulating over—zealous crime reductive mechanisms.

CHAPTER 7

Firearms in the Crime Prevention Equation

Abstract There are some people who take the view that unrestricted access to firearms is an essential tool of crime prevention. This chapter sets out an opposite view: that there is no evidence that guns control crime. Indeed, the evidence is that the presence of a firearm elevates the possibility of fatal harm to innocent victims. The chapter compares data from a gun rich society (the USA) with Australia where gun control is a key political (and well accepted) mandate. It looks at the 1996 post-Port Arthur gun buyback scheme and the gun amnesties that have been legislated since that time. It surmises that Australians are fortunate that the number of legal guns in the community is manageable, and that authorities have implemented appropriate registration and licensing policies that guard against the risk posed by legal and illegal guns. It concludes by listing some recommendations for further reform from the Legal and Constitutional Affairs References Committee of the Australian Parliament.

Keywords Gun ownership · Licensing · Gun registration · Gun deaths · Firearms research

To what extent can easy access to firearms enhance or limit a society's ability to control crime? There are some (notably the US National Rifle Association, or, in Australia, the LDP, now the Libertarian Party) who would say that easy access to firearms is an essential tool of crime prevention (e.g. Lee & Suardi, 2008). Others (e.g. Morris & Hawkins, 1970) would say that reducing access to firearms gives a society the best chance of curtailing violent crime. Let me examine each argument.

It is first worth re-visiting the work of Graham Farrell (2013) on this subject. He examined fifteen hypotheses that had been offered by various commentators to explain the significant drop in crime, especially violent crime, across the Western world since the mid-1990s. The hypotheses he tested included the strategy of placing *more* guns in private hands (hence the ability of private citizens to defend themselves against criminals) and, conversely, a strategy that would have the effect of allowing *fewer* guns to find their way into private hands (hence reducing the likelihood that a gun would be available to a person seeking to engage in criminal conduct). Farrell found no evidence that supported conclusively either proposition as a crime control measure.

However, there is evidence that not only do guns *not* enhance a society's ability to curb crime, their presence also elevates the possibility of harm, indeed, fatal harm. *Ergo*, fewer guns in private hands will have the effect of reducing the possibility that conflicts turn lethal.

In 2013, Bangalore and Messerli published the results of their evaluation of the possible associations between gun ownership rates, mental illness, and firearm-related death. They reviewed the data for 27 developed countries. They concluded that the number of guns per capita per country was a strong and independent predictor of firearm-related deaths (Bangalore & Messerli, 2013).

Likewise, a meta-analysis conducted by Dutch academic John van Kesteren (2014) found as follows:

> In high-gun countries, the risks of escalation to more serious and lethal violence are higher. On balance, considerably more serious crimes of violence are committed in such countries. For this reason, the strict gun-reduction policies of many governments seem to be a sensible means to advance the common good. (van Kesteren, 2014, p. 69)

Van Kesteren presented his analysis of the statistical data to ask whether, at the individual level, a person is safer for having access to a firearm. His study concluded, 'No'. He explained the reasoning thus:

Contrary to what has been claimed by proponents of widespread gun ownership in the United States, those households that own guns run higher risks of seeing their members being criminally victimized, either by other household members or by outsiders who are not deterred from attacking. This correlational finding provides no proof that the higher risks are *caused* by ownership of a gun; ownership might also be a proxy for a high-risk lifestyle. But this result certainly sheds serious doubt on the notion of gun ownership as a protective factor. (van Kesteren, 2014, p. 69, emphasis in the original)

The evidence is growing to support this argument (see Lemieux, 2024; Lemieux et al., 2015). Those who advocate gun ownership as a means of crime prevention are confronting a considerable empirical evidence-based barrier.

There is a suggestion often made by gun advocates that there is a link between the decades-long decline in the US violent crime rate and the prevalence of guns in the hands of American citizens. This suggestion of a causal connection, however, is highly problematic, since violent crime rates have been declining over a similar period (since the mid-1990s) in all industrialised Western democracies, not just the United States, including those countries that have strict gun laws, like Australia. If one is looking for a correlation, one can find it in the number of guns and rates of gun deaths. Comparisons between the United States and Australia are useful here. In 2020, seventy-nine percent of US homicides were committed by firearms (Gramlich, 2022) while in Australia (based on 2019–2020 data) it is 17% (Serpell et al., 2022).

More evidence of the dangers of easy access to firearms is provided by a study from the Harvard School of Public Health, published in 2002. It found that, when it comes to childhood deaths, the ready availability of a firearm makes a great difference to outcomes. Over the period studied (1988–1997), nearly seven thousand American children aged between five and fourteen were killed by a firearm. Children in the five US States with the highest rate of gun ownership (Louisiana, Alabama, Mississippi, Arkansas, and West Virginia) were sixteen times more likely to die from a gun accident than children in the five States with the lowest rate of gun ownership (Hawaii, Massachusetts, Rhode Island, New Jersey, and Delaware). Children in the 'high-gun' States were also seven times more likely to die from a gun suicide and three times more likely to die from a gun homicide. Before an American child reaches fifteen, he or she is twelve times more likely than a child anywhere else in the industrialised world to die of gunshot wounds (Harvard, 2002).

The reasons for this are intuitive, according to researchers Alison Wallace (1986) and David Lester (1990). The presence of a firearm, they affirm, means that low level violence on the street, in the household, or at the workplace can quickly escalate into lethal violence. Suicidal thoughts can quickly become fatal actions; children innocently playing with loaded weapons can quickly become victims; assaults by intimate partners against women in domestic settings can quickly harbour deadly consequences (Eriksson et al., 2022).

On 19 June 2014, the Australian Senate referred the following issue to the Legal and Constitutional Affairs References Committee for their inquiry and report: *The ability of Australian law enforcement authorities to eliminate gun-related violence in the community.* The Committee's report was published on 9 April 2015. There were a number of recommendations, including continued funding for gun monitoring, data sharing, and policies designed to ensure that all firearm data will be transferred to the National Firearms Interface.

Significantly, Recommendation 5 seeks more amnesties:

> The committee recommends that an ongoing, Australia-wide gun amnesty is implemented, with consideration given to ways in which this can be done without limiting the ability of police to pursue investigative leads for serious firearm-related crimes. (Australian Government, 2015)

Of interest was the attention given to the possibility of so-called '3D' gun manufacturing as well, leading to Recommendation 8:

> The committee recommends that Australian governments continue to monitor the risks posed by 3D manufacturing in relation to the manufacture of firearms and consider further regulatory measures if the need arises. (Australian Government, 2015)

The evidence supports the view that high levels of gun violence will continue to persist while people have ready access to guns. In our nation we are fortunate that the numbers of legal guns in the community is manageable, and that authorities have implemented registration and licensing policies that guard against the risk posed by legal guns. Illegal guns and the illicit gun market should thus be highly monitored and eliminated (Bright et al., 2023; Sarre, 1996).

One would hope.

> ... that there will still be sufficient political will to protect and further the major gun law reforms [that have been] achieved... (Chappell, 2014, p. 407)

I cannot leave this topic without some reference here to the considerable attention paid to the regulation of firearms in Australia, over three decades ago, by the National Committee on Violence (NCV) (a unit then within the Australian Institute of Criminology). Their report published in 1990 (National Committee on Violence, 1990) was informed by the fact that three of the NCV's fourteen appointed members were senior law enforcement officers with experience and knowledge of guns and the problems they posed for community safety (Chappell, 2016). There is little doubt that the presence of these officers on the Committee assisted with the development of credible and appropriate recommendations on gun control. However, the pro-gun lobby in Australia was well-organised, well-funded, and determined to oppose any significant reform of gun laws.

Ultimately, the NCV made seventeen recommendations about gun control (National Committee on Violence, 1990, pp. 173–178). In complete unanimity, the Committee members prefaced their proposals for reform with the following statement:

> The two Commissioners of Police who are members of the Committee maintain that a national system of firearms licensing and registration will assist the police in the prevention and control of firearm violence, and will enhance the safety of both the general public and Australian police men and women. On this the entire Committee is in wholehearted agreement, as they are with regard to all of the following recommendations relating to firearms.
>
> The Committee believes that firearm ownership is a privilege, not a right, and that strict controls will impress it upon the public that firearms are inherently dangerous. The Committee urges all Australians to accept that strong measures are needed to deal with the present incidence of gun fatalities and injuries in this country. (National Committee on Violence, 1990, p. 175)

The Committee concluded that 'there is no doubt that significant disarmament of the Australian public would save lives and prevent injury' (National Committee on Violence, 1990, p. 73), and that 'the availability of firearms increases the risk of violent death, both accidental and deliberate' (National Committee on Violence, 1990, p. 74). Accordingly, the Committee recommended (Recommendation 54) the enactment of uniform legislation to regulate the acquisition and possession of firearms, the introduction of uniform guidelines for all police forces on the enforcement of firearms legislation, and the development of a national gun control strategy to reduce the number of firearms and prevent access to them by individuals who are not fit and proper persons. It also recommended (Recommendation 55) that the federal government should prohibit the sale of surplus military weapons, prohibit the importation of military style weapons for use other than by law enforcement officers, prohibit the sale of mail order firearms, and bring rifle clubs established under the *Defence Act* within State and Territory licensing requirements.

The response of Australian governments to these recommendations was decidedly lukewarm. Six years later, however, on April 28, 1996, a massacre at Port Arthur erupted. It changed everything (Chapman, 1998; Sarre, 2019b). Gun control under the Howard Liberal government (which had only been in office for seven weeks) took a serious turn. The buyback scheme compensated gun owners who surrendered 650,000 firearms at a cost of $367 million (Sarre, 2019c). The political imperative to keep guns out of the hands of those who do not need them continues today with bipartisan political support.

There is little doubt that all Australian parliaments will continue to exhibit strong political leadership on restrictive gun policies for the foreseeable future. There is no evidence that a more widespread availability of guns in the hands of the public would make any difference to crime control, and indeed, on the evidence presented above, having more guns available and lifting the current restrictions would make matters worse.

CHAPTER 8

Corrections and Crime Prevention

Abstract This chapter explores the dramatic rise in prisoner numbers over the last four decades in Australia and determines that that rise is having a counter-productive effect on crime prevention notwithstanding its short-term incapacitative effect. It sets out the findings of the Productivity Commission in 2021 that highlighted the opportunity costs associated with imprisonment. It explains the 'restorative' justice mechanisms that are available to judges and magistrates today as alternatives to custodial options. It mentions the evidence that citizens are not opposed to alternatives to prison (such as community service and probation) in circumstances where there is little risk to public safety. It highlights the deleterious effects of imprisonment on society generally (beyond the massive financial cost) and the shameful over-representation of First Nations men and women in custody, highlighted most recently in the work of the Justice Reform Initiative, a national campaign with bipartisan support. The chapter concludes with the rejection of any notion that 'nothing works' in rehabilitation.

Keyword Incarceration rates · Opportunity costs · Pre and post-release services · Youth detention centres · Aboriginal courts

There is little doubt that Australia's custodial landscape is changing: our prisoner numbers have increased dramatically over the last four decades. Federal Labor politician Andrew Leigh speculated in 2019 on the causes:

> Since 1985, the Australian incarceration rate has risen by 130 percent, and now stands at 0.22 percent of adults, its highest level since Federation. …The recent increase in the Australian prison population does not seem to be due to crime rates, which have mostly fallen over the past generation. Instead, higher reporting rates, stricter policing practices, tougher sentencing laws, and more stringent bail laws appear to be the main drivers of Australia's growing prison population. (Leigh, 2019, p. 1)

This trend continues to this day. As at June 30, 2023 there were almost 42,000 prisoners in Australia, an increase of 3% over the previous 12 months (ABS, 2024). That is a rate of 202 adult prisoners per 100,000 population.

The issue of the consequences of a growing Australian imprisonment rate was addressed in a Productivity Commission (2021) report. Its Executive Summary includes the following observation:

> [T]he level of imprisonment has changed due to changes in the level and mix of crime. There has been an increase in some types of serious crime, such as sexual assault and drug trafficking. But there has also been a decrease in other types of serious crime such as homicide and robbery. There is also evidence of increased reporting of crime, which raises the level of imprisonment. … [Moreover]… in a number of states and territories, policies have made bail harder to access and remand the default position for a wide range of offences. Also, many jurisdictions have introduced prison-based mandatory sentencing. These policy changes mean that, for a given rate of crime, more people will spend more time in prison. (Productivity Commission, 2021, p. 3)

A key reason for the rise in imprisonment, identified by both Leigh and the authors of the Productivity Commission report, is the fact that nowadays bail is harder to access. Remand in custody has become, for the most part, the default position for a wide range of offences across all jurisdictions. 15,937 of Australian prisoners (38%) in 2023 were unsentenced, almost all of whom were on remand awaiting trial (ABS, 2024).

The consequences of such a restrictive bail policy have been known for years (Morris & Hawkins, 1970; Sarre & Bartels, 2023; Travers et al.,

2020). That is an untenable and costly position for any government to be in.

There is no doubt that the incapacitation of people who are locked up, and thus unable to commit crime, can be a factor in reducing criminal conduct. Indeed, there is a related argument that general deterrence (the threat of that same penalty being applied for a similar offence) plays a role here too. But what is forgotten by anyone making such an assertion is that there is a very high opportunity cost associated with imprisonment, an observation that has a long history (e.g. Tomasic & Dobinson, 1979). Every dollar that Australian governments (State, Territory, and Federal) spend on drawing people into, and keeping people in, the corrections system is potentially a dollar that could have been spent on initiatives that have been shown to stem the flow of potential offenders into the formal justice processes in the first place. These initiatives include employment incentives, educational opportunities, Indigenous mentoring, community capacity-building, drug treatments, mental health programs, diversionary processes, post-release services (including housing and employment for those leaving prison), affordable public housing, therapeutic (problem-solving) courts, Aboriginal community courts, and interventions for 'at risk' individuals and their families (McCausland & Baldry, 2023; NSW Department of Communities and Justice, 2023).

What are known as 'restorative' justice options and mechanisms need mention here too. They have made a significant and beneficial mark on international justice processes in the last thirty years (Braithwaite, 1996), including in Australia (Richards, 2009; Sarre & Young, 2011) and especially New Zealand where Canadian and United States model initiatives developed in the 1970s took root in magistrates and youth courts dealing with juvenile and young adult crime, especially among Māori (Marshall, 2015, 2020). These mechanisms include restorative justice 'conferencing' for young people who have come to the attention of the police, with options available in the adult courts, too, at the behest of innovative judges and magistrates (McCold, 2001), and in policing and correctional services and practices (Sarre, 1999).

Intriguingly, governments do spend significant amounts of money on all of these programs, but they seem reluctant to advertise the fact, perhaps because it might look like they are assisting lawbreakers whom many in the wider community would class as 'the undeserving'. No politician wants to look like they are soft on crime. This is an odd and expensive political disconnect (Sarre, 2011).

The literature on incarceration, too, has consistently revealed the downsides of an emphasis upon using custodial options to forge citizen compliance with the law. What is forgotten in the deterrence equation (and needs to be factored into any such response) is the physical and psychological hardship placed upon the prisoner; the assaults and deaths in custody; the implications financially for their families; the deleterious effects on their children; the criminogenic effect of mixing sentenced prisoners with remandees; the paucity of programs available for those who find themselves locked up, and the limited evidence of any deterrent effect on those imprisoned for short periods (Wan & Weatherburn, 2022).

The over-representation of First Nations men and women in custody has been a national and international embarrassment for many years (Kelly & Tubex, 2015). First Nations Australians represent just over three percent of the total population, yet a third of the prison population identifies as First Nations (ABS, 2024; Korff, 2022). And from July 2002 to June 2023, First Nations Australians made up a quarter of the deaths in custody (Productivity Commission, 2024b, Table 8A.17).

The current data on youth detention are eye-opening and disturbing, too. On an average day if one were to visit children's detention centres, one would find 72 percent of the children held there are unsentenced (AIHW, 2022). In 2023–2024 in Australia the average nightly population of children aged 10–17 who were in detention was 794 (Productivity Commission, 2024b, Table 17A.2). Sixty-three percent of these children were First Nations (Productivity Commission, 2024b, Table 17A.5). The flow-through data show the picture of the over-use of imprisonment for unsentenced children (Halsey & Deegan, 2015). Ninety seven percent of children received into custody in 2020/2021 were unsentenced. And ninety percent of children released from custody were released from unsentenced detention. Thirty six percent of unsentenced children completed their remand period and received some form of sentence. But of this cohort, only a fifth went on to be sentenced to detention.

Moreover, Donald Ritchie asserts that high levels of custodial rates may be criminogenic:

> Sentences of imprisonment exert a significant incapacitative effect on offenders for the duration of their imprisonment. The findings from studies into incapacitation, however, suggest that a system of collective incapacitation that increases the use of imprisonment or the length of prison terms without distinguishing between offenders who exhibit varying degrees of

risk of future offending will generally be ineffective in achieving significant long-term reductions in crime. The findings indicate that the costs of such policies may outweigh the initial benefits, and that, as the imprisonment rate increases, those benefits may even be reversed to a point where the crime rate begins to increase due to the criminogenic influence of imprisonment. (Ritchie, 2012, p. 2)

Few commentators challenge the assumption that punitiveness is what citizens want. In contrast, there is good research evidence that the average voter, when given complete information, is not as punitive or vindictive as we might think or fear. Studies done in Victoria by the Sentencing Advisory Council (SAC) found that respondents, when asked a simple abstract question about sentencing practices generally, expressed the view that judges and magistrates are too lenient. But when given more information about the crime and about an offender, respondents' levels of punitiveness drop dramatically. Karen Gelb concluded that, when given complete information, people are willing to accept alternatives to imprisonment. Indeed, and perhaps counter-intuitively, they found that victims of crime were no more punitive than others (Gelb, 2011).

It is undeniable that in prisons, remand centres, and police cells we find principally those who are economically marginalised and facing labour market uncertainty, and who live under the influence of drugs, poor education, or mental illness.

The proportion of offenders with a history of mental illness is over 50 percent and that figure is even higher for young people in custody. Almost 90 percent of young people in custody have a past or present psychological disorder. The estimates of prisoners with intellectual disability or borderline intellectual disability are as high as 20 percent. All these people have limited access to appropriate mental health or other critical support while they are in prison, and most will be released back into the community in a relatively short period of time. (Justice Reform Initiative, 2020, pp. 1–2)

To borrow from Reiman (2007), the rich get richer, and the poor get prison.

When they are released (and more than the current daily number of our nation's prisoners on any one night are released each year), inmates find that many of the problems they were dealing with upon sentence persist or have been compounded. The authors of the briefing papers for the Justice Reform Initiative describe the consequences.

> Only a quarter of inmates are entering adult prison for the first time and more than half return within two years. Overcrowding is making it difficult to provide proper training and support programs to help prevent people leaving jail from re-offending and can actually make them more likely to commit further crimes. (Justice Reform Initiative, 2020, p. 1)

Here is what the authors conclude on the subject of youth detention.

> Sadly, most of the young people in Australia's juvenile justice system come from backgrounds where they have already often suffered from severe neglect or abuse and/or have been placed in out of home care. This was clearly demonstrated by the Royal Commission into the Don Dale Centre in the Northern Territory. The children in these centres, who can be as young as 10, have often had the hardest of young lives and need family and community support, education and life opportunities, rather than being locked up. (Justice Reform Initiative, 2020, p. 2)

It is important in this context to review the oft-made assertion that 'nothing works?' in rehabilitative practice in corrections (Sarre, 2001). The phrase was coined almost fifty years ago after social scientist Robert Martinson published a paper in the journal *The Public Interest* entitled 'What Works? – Questions and Answers About Prison Reform' (Martinson, 1974). The take-away from the publication was that very little worked. It is important to note, however, that Martinson was only one of three researchers to undertake a survey of rehabilitation programs and their effectiveness, which was published as *The Effectiveness of Correctional Treatment* (Lipton et al., 1975). The survey had been completed in 1970 but was not publicly released until five years later. Although the results came to be essentially identified with Martinson's name alone, he had joined the other two only after they were well into their work. Unknown to co-authors Doug Lipton and Judith Wilks, Martinson published the now famous article peremptorily and without their consent (Lipton, 1998).

The final 735-page report, published just six months after the appearance of the Martinson article, concluded that 'the field of corrections has not as yet found satisfactory ways to reduce recidivism by significant amounts' (Lipton et al., 1975). This was a far more guarded conclusion. It left open the door for further rehabilitative optimism. The three authors appeared keen to emphasise that one should not shut the door on rehabilitation without first developing better diagnostic evaluative tools and collecting better data. As Gendreau and Ross noted some years later,

> [a]ll too often, in the face of all contrary empirical evidence, we adhere to theories for political or ideological reasons ... or cavalierly switch ideologies depending upon transient political developments ... (Gendreau & Ross, 1987, p. 395)

In Australia, we have long put paid to any suggestion that 'nothing works'. For example, contemporary understandings of child development are increasingly being recognised as both relevant and important to the way in which the community works with justice-involved children and young people (Malvaso et al., 2024). Modern interpretations of Australia's human rights obligations inform services that are provided to those who are victims of international crimes such as human trafficking (Marmo & Chazal, 2010).

Moreover, there has been a rejection of 'nothing works' in Australia and, in contrast, a celebration of good programming in rehabilitative settings within prisons. However, these programs, generally speaking, remain under-funded, are not uniformly legislated, and have few public champions (Howells et al., 2004; Heseltine et al., 2011). Indeed, while lip-service is paid to the goal of rehabilitation in official sentencing policies, much of the terminology is ambiguous. For example, even though Sect. 5 of the Victorian *Sentencing Act 1991* states that one of the purposes for which sentences may be imposed is to 'establish conditions within which it is considered by the court that the rehabilitation of the offender may be facilitated', the legislation speaks in passive rather than active voice. In other jurisdictions, other factors are given pre-eminence in sentencing guidelines. In South Australia, for example, the *Criminal Law (Sentencing) Act 1988* was repealed and replaced in 2017 to prescribe that the primary purpose for sentencing a defendant in that State is 'to protect the safety of the community'. Hence, while rehabilitation has never completely faded as a justification for punishment, and while the interpretation of the verb 'to protect' remains moot (Livings, 2021), a deserts-based approach holds a pre-eminent place in contemporary South Australian sentencing practices.

There have been, however, some pleasing developments in recent years. The first is the creation of specialist courts, installed under the broad title of therapeutic justice, sometimes referred to as therapeutic jurisprudence (Freiberg, 2003; Winick & Wexler, 2004). These include drug courts currently operating in all States, where treatment and rehabilitation are given a primary focus (Oleson, 2017; Sarre & Daly, 2021), along with mental health courts, family and domestic violence courts in some jurisdictions, and Aboriginal courts that operate across the country under various names (such as Murri courts in Queensland) where the emphasis is upon restoration and remediation (Bennett, 2015; Marchetti, 2014).

The second development worth noting is prison privatisation. While privatisation continues to arouse intense suspicion and antipathy especially in the United States (Bauer, 2018; Dreisinger, 2016), and while there is little doubt that private self-interest can intrude into Australian private prison business decision-making, it remains the case that private contractors are required to set and sustain certain performance indicators regarding rehabilitation or else suffer financial penalties (Harding, 1997, p. 19). Tim Prenzler and I reviewed the evidence on modern prison privatisation in this country in 2021 (Sarre & Prenzler, 2021b). We were of the view that to improve accountability, protocols need to be put in place to ensure genuine independence on the part of prison inspectors and others who audit prison practices (see Crime and Corruption Commission, 2018). Indeed, in Queensland, the Auditor-General made a number of recommendations that included a more 'outcome-focused performance management system' and 'assessing the fraud risk that operators could overstate their performance' (Queensland Audit Office, 2016, p. 6).

As the Productivity Commission concluded in 2021, Australians need to ask themselves if current prison policy is providing the best value outcomes for Australia. And, if not, what are the alternatives that we should be trialling to get better value for taxpayers' money (Productivity Commission, 2021).

Policymakers are attracted to prisons because building them gives the public a tangible thing to look at. True, prisons provide some deterrent effect on some crimes for some people, and there is certainly a short-term incapacitative effect, but an over-reliance upon prison as a crime reduction strategy comes at a significant financial cost, is not consistent across offences nor jurisdictions, ruins family life for the children of prisoners, and is inequitable in terms of the people who finds themselves there. Targeted custodial options (for example, for a convicted offender intent on terrorist acts) need to be placed into the criminal justice 'mix'.

And whatever the cost, governments should be providing a full suite of health services in custodial settings, particularly concerning mental health.

Any suggestion that Australians must rely upon high imprisonment rates as a bulwark against crime needs to be challenged and, on the current evidence, disregarded.

CHAPTER 9

Avoiding Political Interference in Crime Prevention

Abstract This chapter examines the role that ill-conceived political imperatives play in damaging the crime prevention task. Governments do not want to have anyone say that they are 'soft on crime' and so they employ language that encourages voters to think that short-term 'justice system' responses are the only way to ensure community safety. The chapter challenges that approach. It speaks to the value of the campaign for legislatures to raise the age of criminal responsibility, to expand the use of pill testing at festivals, and to embrace the idea of 'justice reinvestment'. It notes the evidence that politicians are wrong when they think that the voting public is suspicious of rehabilitation programs. It calls out the reluctance of governments to link social justice spending to lower crime rates lest they give the impression that their parsimony is criminogenic. The chapter concludes with the admonition for our society to engage in well-informed debates free from penal populism.

Keywords Political imperatives · Criminogenic effects · Age of criminal responsibility · Justice reinvestment · Penal populism

Decades of valuable criminological research reinforce the clear message that there are preferred paths that need to be taken by communities, by governments, and by private and not-for-profit organisations, in the pursuit of more secure communities and lower rates of crime and fear of crime. We now have a large and growing body of criminological literature, datasets, and other statistical information all of which allow us to consider the best options for the delivery of a crime-reduced nation and for a palatable price. This literature can direct us and thereby allow us to avoid the consequences of governments acting too hastily in the rush to be seen as 'doing something' about crime and the fear of crime (Ayling, 2013).

However, there are suspicions that the preferred options that have been tested and recommended by the researchers are often supervened by political imperatives. Let me offer two examples:

1. The research evidence points to the harm-reductive benefits of a supervised drug injecting room for addicts who need a safe place for their (ostensibly illegal) behaviour, attracting addicts prepared to present for help rather than to seek criminogenic means to feed to their addiction. A government keen to be seen to 'doing something' about drugs, however, is not likely to embrace these evidentiary nostrums.
2. The research evidence points to the criminogenic effects of imprisonment, but governments, keen to be seen to be 'doing something' about the apparent rise in the incidence of certain criminal behaviour, will, more often than not, simply raise the penalties (most often lengthening carceral terms) for that behaviour.

The work of Carol Bacchi (2012) is helpful here. She talks about rethinking strategic options by challenging the representation of the problem. For example, if the problem is represented to be a growing incidence of crime in the community, this will generate a certain political expectation and then there will be pressure placed on governments to enact a certain response. If the problem is represented, in contrast, as a consequence of social inequality and disadvantage that limit outcomes for families and individuals, the expectations and responses will be different.

In 1991 I wrote the following words, somewhat despairingly, in highlighting how Australia could reduce levels of violence in the community.

> The implementation of initiatives derived from social science research requires Ministers of State with imagination, intellect, enthusiasm and

energy, characteristics that are all too often lacking in political life. Typically, social science data is used in the "symbolic" sense by politicians quick to score political points while catching their opponents off guard, or in circumstances where a response is needed in order to maintain credibility in a crisis. (Sarre, 1991, p. 271)

Sadly, not much appears to have changed in the last thirty years, notwithstanding that our knowledge of the problems and the evidence-based prophylactic tools at our disposal have grown exponentially. There are, however, some areas that give us hope that the message is finally getting through.

A recent example is the strong push around Australia currently to raise the age of criminal responsibility to 14 (McLachlan, 2023; Moulds & Krishna, 2020). The Northern Territory and the Australian Capital Territory raised the age of criminal responsibility from 10 to 12 in 2023, and Victoria in 2024, while the ACT will raise the age to 14 in 2025. South Australia is considering raising the age to 12 in the near future (Canny, 2022). This is an admirable quest, given the criminogenic effect of detaining, questioning, and imprisoning young people (Cunneen & Rowe, 2014).

Another example is the campaign to expand the use of pill testing at festivals as a way of keeping those who might be attracted to consuming illicit drugs safe from harm (Alcohol and Drug Foundation, 2021; Barratt et al., 2019).

In order to expose the fallacies and to turn the naysaying 'ship' around, there are, to my mind, three challenges:

1. Opposition spokespersons need to open up a debate rather than be (to borrow from the names given to the identical twins in Lewis Carroll's *Alice in Wonderland*) Tweedledee to the government's Tweedledum. Having a timid Opposition that agrees with everything the government says on law-and-order issues does not make for good policymaking.
2. Policymakers need to disabuse themselves of the assumption that punitiveness is what citizens want. The evidence is there that, when given the right information, the population is not as punitive or vindictive as our political leaders might think or fear.
3. Researchers need to drive home the argument that a safe community is one that is built on trust, equality of opportunity, and social

capital, not one where those who do not sit comfortably inside the 'norm' are simply locked away.

Peter Norden's book *Seeking Justice* addresses well the phenomenon of political interference and indifference in criminal justice policies (Norden, 2021). He refers to the work of the late Tony Vinson, the lead researcher on the study published as *Unequal in Life: the distribution of social disadvantage in Victoria and New South Wales* (Vinson, 1999). Professor Vinson looked at postcodes (locality) and how they correlated with disadvantage. The conclusion of Vinson was that a range of social indicators —low income, poor housing, domestic violence, long-term unemployment, social exclusion, young adults not fully engaged in work or study, poor health, early school leaving, and criminal convictions—contribute independently to disadvantage and are interwoven. Indeed, if crime and disadvantage are inter-related, says Norden, it is 'lop-sided' to favour funding the former—the mechanisms of criminal justice—while paying scant attention to the latter (Norden, 2021, pp. 303–304). He argues as follows:

> [This] is why the repeated, frustrated calls for a change in approach that I have been arguing for ... should again be reconsidered today: an approach that redirects the resources from the construction and ongoing operation of a rapidly expanding prison estate to one which draws on the evidence and redirects a percentage of those resources to those communities that have been mined more and more deeply by the instrumentalities of the criminal justice system: *justice reinvestment*. (Norden, 2021, p. 317, emphasis in the original)

Governments (and oppositions) of all persuasions usually remain quiet on these issues because they are unsure about whether touting social initiatives (as opposed to their 'law and order' credentials) will jeopardise their political survival (Sarre, 2009). Contrast the strong commitment of all governments to end domestic and familial violence focusing on prophylactic measures that are not underpinned by tougher approaches to sentencing (Australian Government, 2023b). The Senate weighed into this argument positively a decade ago (Australian Government, 2013). Governments have been known to highlight their credentials in pumping resources into mental health programs and drug and alcohol rehabilitation. Moreover, on 1 February 2024, the Albanese government announced that it had committed $79 million to supporting up to thirty community-led justice reinvestment initiatives in First Nations communities across Australia.

All of these commitments are applauded. It is odd that governments tend to display enormous timidity when it comes to linking these funding initiatives to advance the aim of lowering crime rates. They could easily tout this spending as a crime prevention initiative. Their reluctance to do so is troubling.

It is imperative for all modern societies to find effective strategies to protect victims, to stop victimisation, and to stem the tide of people who keep coming to the attention of police. It is imperative that we reinvest the dollars that would otherwise have been spent on formal justice processes into these strategies. That will not happen without well-informed debates free from the politics of 'law-and-order' populism (Antolak-Saper, 2023).

American criminologist Elliott Currie in this context refers to 'transformative intervention'.

> ... I want to counterpose what lately I've been calling 'transformative' intervention: in other words, intervention designed not to try to fit people into the existing structure of the society around them, but to engage them in the process of transforming themselves by working to *challenge* the conditions that now diminish and distort their lives. Transformative intervention involves helping people to move beyond the individualistic, often exploitative, often uncaring cultural orientations that now suffuse their communities – and our society as a whole – and to begin to relate differently to themselves, to those around them, and to the larger community (and the planet): to nurture alternative ways of looking at the world and their place in it that, among other things, will be less violent, less predatory and less exploitative. (Currie, 2013, p. 6, emphasis in the original)

I am of the view that researchers need to tell governments and their spokespersons that they *can* build long-term social investment into criminal justice policymaking without risking electoral backlash. They need to broadcast the relevant evidence, and explain the research results, and how they are acting upon them. They need not fear voter reproach. There is reason to suspect that the community is ready for such debates and results, and will not punish at the polls any party brave enough to raise them.

Having said that, and as I was thinking about this topic in January 2024, a letter to the editor of the local newspaper in Adelaide caught my attention. The author wrote, 'Does anybody else think we could dissuade criminals from committing crimes if there were no minimum sentences—just maximums, and that were applied universally, without exception, to every crime? Worth a try?' The ignorance expressed here is disturbing. Our politicians need to be aware of the challenges presented by voters who resort to tired and dated assumptions, ignorant of the research evidence. These politicians cannot afford to ignore the views of the general public, but they must present the case for a different approach, and have the courage of their convictions in doing so.

CHAPTER 10

Future Directions Required of All of Us

Abstract This chapter summarises what we know and what we now need to do to reduce crime. Given the research evidence that, fortunately, expands daily, we do know a great deal about what works in crime prevention, what complicates matters, and whom policymakers should be listening to and whom they should be ignoring in putting programs and strategies in place. We know, too, what often frustrates the task, namely the criminal justice system itself. It too often gets in the way, yet pretends that it is essential to the task. The chapter repeats observations made by many criminologists about what should be the key focus of crime prevention, namely that our society needs to devote far more attention to the wellbeing of children, preventing their abuse and neglect, and trumpeting the importance of eradicating the intergenerational trauma that continues to supply young candidates for police attention. It concludes with a plea that policymakers adopt evidence-based solutions and reject 'quick fixes'.

Keywords State resourcing · Social disadvantage · School failure · Child abuse · Child neglect

Let me summarise what we know, drawn from the above pages. We know that police are an important component in crime reduction, but they are only one very small part of the crime control landscape. We know that cooperative policing arrangements with the private sector have been very successful in limiting criminal opportunities, but these arrangements carry their own concerns, especially regarding adequate training and accountability. We know that the zeal of policymakers to reduce corporate crime is undeniable, but the idea of going further and extending criminal attribution by reference to the culture of the corporate body has not been sufficiently embraced by Australian parliaments, and nor has it been tested in the courts of the jurisdiction where a 'culture' approach has been legislated. We know that the work of justice agencies engaged to track down and prosecute those who would commit financial crimes is zealous, but the threat of imprisonment appears to be having no deterrent effect upon the perpetrators. We know that increased surveillance is an important tool in crime control, but we need to ensure that it is our servant, not our master. We know that having access to personal data is important in the fight against terrorism, but the data retention scheme and other surveillance strategies are expensive, and we have no way of determining whether they are having the desired effect. We know that a society that employs strong gun controls is a less lethal society, but gun control is difficult to manage politically when gun owners argue for their legitimate needs. Finally, we know that imprisonment has an important containment effect, but it is a very crude, expensive, and potentially counter-productive weapon in the crime control arsenal.

We thus know a great deal about what works to assist the crime prevention task, and what complicates and frustrates the task. If that were not a difficult enough weighing—up exercise, we are also constantly being distracted. Governments of all persuasions like to reinforce in the public's mind that properly resourcing police, prosecutions, courts, and corrections are the sole keys to public safety. It is not surprising, then, that every time some tragic event occurs there is an outcry that 'something must be done about it', and people in political life (regardless of their political stripe) will suggest increasing the numbers and powers of police, lifting the rates of imprisonment, and lengthening the terms of incarceration.

Criminologists are then asked to comment, and as soon as they say (correctly) that there is no 'silver bullet' to crime reduction, politicians, policymakers, and the public all tend to turn off, and retreat to their 'police, courts and corrections' solutions mantra. I encourage criminologists to keep talking notwithstanding, and policymakers to keep listening. For while there are many complexities to the causes of and solutions to crime (Baldry, 2013) there are nevertheless preferred options to the crime reduction puzzle, and they can all be found in the available evidence.

Let me make some observations, and offer some preferred options.

In February 2017, I delivered a keynote address at the Applied Research in Crime and Justice Conference, jointly convened by the NSW Bureau of Crime Statistics and Research and the Griffith Criminology Institute (Sarre, 2017). My words were designed to shift the gaze of policymakers from responding *after* the crime event to the factors that may have precipitated it.

I pointed to the watershed Australian study entitled Pathways to Prevention (Developmental Crime Prevention Consortium, 1999), conducted a quarter century ago, but still cited widely today (Homel, 2021). It showed that strategies that involve specialists interceding with protective factors (positive interactions) at crucial developmental transition points in a young person's life (when they are 'vulnerable' to such intervention) can have the effect of reducing law-breaking. According to the researchers, the reinforcement of these effects is dependent upon a community's capacity to agree on goals for a child's well-being and its ability to mobilise efforts to meet them (Homel et al., 2015).

I referred to a longitudinal study in New Zealand that revealed something similar. The Christchurch Health and Development Study, a 35-year study of a birth cohort of 1,265 children born in the Christchurch region in the mid-1970s, revealed much about the importance of crime prevention of proper social and psychological development of children (Fergusson et al., 2015). Developmental criminology and life-course criminology studies have set out strategies for policymakers that draw down from this research (McGee & Mazerolle, 2015), emphasising that the key is early intervention (Piquero et al., 2016) that forestalls the intergenerational trauma that continues to supply candidates for police attention.

I reminded conference-goers that theorists have been exploring for decades the links between social disadvantage and crime. There is now a large and growing inventory of literature that details the criminality wrought by inequality, racial disharmony, and economic impediment (Deckert, 2016; Marchetti, 2015; Waretini-Karena, 2017; Wilkinson & Pickett, 2009). A study that was conducted over ten years in Australia showed that variations in income levels have a greater effect on crime rates than any shift in the intensity of policing or deterrent sentences (Wan et al., 2012).

I cited a randomised trial in the United States that was published in 2008 that reported on the progress of children born to mothers with 'low psychological resources' (as the researchers referred to them) and who were living in highly disadvantaged settings. One group of children received specialist services by nurses. By the age of 12, these children were less likely to engage in substance abuse and to suffer mental health problems. Their academic achievements also improved (Olds, 2008). After a follow-up study (Olds et al., 2014), the authors concluded that the program was a promising means of reducing all-cause mortality among mothers and preventable-cause mortality of their first-born children.

I pointed to the evidence in the United States of a direct link between child abuse and violent crime, and between school failure and crime (Currie, 1998, 2008). Australian studies, too, from over thirty years ago, revealed that children with substantiated records of physical abuse and neglect are more likely to be arrested earlier in childhood than those who do not have such records (Weatherburn & Lind, 1997, 1998). Indeed, a more recent study surveyed 8,500 Australians to obtain self-reported data on all five child maltreatment types (physical abuse, sexual abuse, emotional abuse, neglect, and exposure to domestic violence) and criminal justice system involvement. It reported that one in twelve maltreated women and one in four maltreated men reported at least one arrest during their lives, compared to one in twenty-five non-maltreated women and one in eight non-maltreated men (Mathews et al., 2023; Haslam et al., 2023).

I noted the studies that asserted that abuse, neglect, intergenerational trauma, and family violence are significantly associated with the alcohol and drug dependence of children's caregivers (Payne & Gaffney, 2012). One study went so far as to suggest that governments should limit the availability of cheap packaged wine, and place restrictions on the number of alcohol licences permitted in selected neighbourhoods (Livingston, 2011; see also Donnelly et al., 2015). These findings are not dissimilar to those of a study in a First Nations setting (Boffa et al., 2018).

What can we conclude from all of these themes and data? It is that the task of crime prevention and reduction requires a multi-faceted response and involves a careful selection of strategies. A successful crime prevention outcome is dependent upon the nature of the offence, the characteristics of offenders, the geographic location of the offence, and the response to the offence by the state. Outcomes may be dependent upon which government (state, federal, or local) is the key driver of the program or initiative designed to reduce crime, and whether the implementation of the program has been properly or poorly managed. The good news is that the evidence needed to sift the wheat from the chaff both in content and delivery is available. My plea is that policymakers use it in their strategic decision-making and funding. We can then reduce the amount of government spending on crime and justice responses in Australia, currently over $23 billion annually (Productivity Commission, 2024c, Table CA.1).

That should not be too much to ask, and think of the savings that will be made.

CHAPTER 11

My Twelve Imperatives

Abstract This final chapter contains my twelve key imperatives for policymakers, not one of which involves expanding the criminal justice mechanisms (police, prosecutions, courts, and corrections) that are usually described by political voices as the only means to defeat crime and general lawlessness. The chapter adopts the idea, proffered by Morris and Hawkins in their 1970 book, that 'honest politicians' can and should do something about crime from a social justice perspective. That will not happen unless and until they have the courage of their convictions. The chapter explains how every dollar poorly spent in the crime reductive quest is the result of a deliberate political choice, and that dollar is then no longer available for the preferred and evidence-based options. The chapter concludes with the oft repeated (and accurate) axiom that society cannot arrest and imprison its way out of crime. Our political leaders must lead, not follow, in promoting this axiom.

Keywords Cultural approaches · Human rights · Diversionary pathways · Skills training

From all of the readings and the evidence contained herein, I present my twelve key strategic imperatives and the preferred choices we need to make in order to reduce crime. In the spirit of the Morris and Hawkins quest (referred to earlier in this book), I direct these imperatives to the attention of (using the Morris and Hawkins terminology) 'honest politicians' by way of a series of 'ukases' (decrees). In 1970 Morris and Hawkins listed 45 ukases, scattered throughout their chapters. My list is more modest, containing just twelve key imperatives. Note that not one of them mentions expanding the justice mechanisms (police, prosecutions, courts, and corrections) that are currently in place (and that usually appear in political parlance and in letters to editors published in the popular press) as the means to defeat crime.

Our governments, national, state, and local (and, where appropriate, in concert with the non-government sector) must:

1. provide police training regarding the important role of police in crime reduction including focusing on procedural justice as a fundamental precept of successful policing;
2. integrate public police and private security agencies in joint policing enterprises with a clear understanding of roles, rights, and legal powers;
3. champion the legislative possibilities alive in using a 'culture' approach to the eradication of corporate wrongdoing rather than adopting an *ex post facto* deterrence model that has been shown to be largely ineffective;
4. explore and employ the tools of surveillance that have been shown to be effective in crime (especially cybercrime) reduction while ensuring through legislation the mandating of transparency of use with a keen regard for human rights;
5. hold the line on the strong gun laws that currently pertain in Australia for the national registration of firearms and licensing of firearm owners;
6. increase funding for pre- and post-release correctional programs, while introducing reforms that will reduce the number of people in prison, especially First Nations Australians;
7. protect victims of domestic and family violence by generously funding shelters and support networks and providing legal and welfare advice;
8. continue to encourage diversionary pathways and restorative justice mechanisms for young people who come to the attention of police, and expand these restorative justice options into the adult courts;

9. instil protective and empowering factors in all young people's lives by funding more generously education, mental health services, mentoring, and skills training;
10. champion an expansion of the use of therapeutic (problem-solving) courts and explain their effectiveness to the public;
11. lift up First Nations justice reforms, and, given the high proportion of First Nations young people currently in youth detention centres, raise the age of criminal responsibility to at least 12 and potentially 14;
12. address social and economic disadvantage in Australia, prioritising social policies that focus on mental health, community housing, broad educational pathways and employment opportunities.

True, culpable defendants must be held accountable. But to get the best outcome for public safety, one must prevent the misconduct in the first place, and give social determinants prominence in that endeavour. To recite a useful metaphor that is repeated over and over in crime reduction literature, it is far better to place a fence at the top of the cliff rather than an ambulance at the bottom of the cliff.

Does the presentation of the above strategies imply that I see the world divided into those who offend and those who do not? No, not at all. Sometimes people drift alongside criminality, take risks with it, and choose to engage in it of their own volition when circumstances present themselves. There are preventative strategies designed to deter these individuals. But it is my view that, for the most part, people fall into crime when social controls break down, or when the vicissitudes of life present no credible alternatives. In these instances there is good evidence that those lives can be turned around before (and after) the offending occurs, with the appropriate allocation of social, psychological, and financial resources.

Those expenditures present as a far better use of our justice dollars than simply raising penalties and employing more police to enforce more punitive laws. We need to reinvest a significant proportion of the resources currently going into police, prosecutions, courts, and corrections into prevention of the factors that drive up crime rates (Australian Government, 2013; Norden, 2021).

How do we pay for this? The government funds bucket is not inexhaustible. Neither is the supply of human service professionals limitless. It *is* a zero sum game. Every dollar poorly spent in the justice quest is the result of a deliberate political choice, and that dollar is then no longer available for other choices. A choice may be between building a new prison or spending on programs designed to give employment incentives to men and women who are leaving prison. It may be between hiring more police or providing more educational opportunities to young people whose lives are in or heading into dysfunctional settings. The important point to make is that the evidence to assist with each of these choices is available to budget-tight government bureaucrats.

If accompanied by enough political momentum, even modest budgetary allocations devoted to social justice initiatives can drive down crime rates. Law-and-order politics, in contrast, provides an expensive disconnect, and one that will guarantee that the problems associated with crime today will be revisited on our children and their children's children.

To help policymakers in their choices quest, I quote from a speech delivered by Australia's first federal Human Rights Commissioner, Brian Burdekin AO when he was awarded an honorary doctorate from the University of South Australia at the 2014 graduation ceremonies. He challenged the assembled graduate classes:

> ...to be conscious of the obligations we all share – both professionally and personally – to create a culture of human rights, of tolerance, of non-discrimination, of respect for individual differences, and one in which the rights of the most vulnerable and disadvantaged in our country are respected and protected. ...Never forget that the birthright you have enjoyed in this enormously fortunate country and the privilege you have of a higher education give you the opportunity and responsibility to help those less fortunate than yourselves. (Burdekin, 2014)

A quotation attributed to Albert Einstein captures this dual challenge of information and responsibility. Paraphrasing him, I remind readers that those who have the privilege to know have the duty to act. That responsibility needs to be accepted and acted upon now.

These obligations give rise to important debates. Careful deliberations are needed to shift us away from the short-term thinking that governments too often promote. Let me assert what every evidence-based crime prevention advocate knows implicitly: we cannot arrest and imprison our way out of crime. We must be better and smarter than that.

CHAPTER 12

Conclusion

Abstract This final chapter observes that if we do not meet the challenges and grab with both hands the options and programs listed in this book, greater expenditures will be required to pay for the losses due to crime and victimisation that await us in the future. In other words, it is better to pay up front now rather than foist these additional expenditures upon our grandchildren. There is enough money to expend now, of course, for the criminal justice system is a very expensive system indeed. Reinvesting that money into crime prevention programs that work is a far better approach. The chapter concludes that we have clear choices in relation to crime reduction and prevention that are achievable, cost-effective, and realistic so long as we maintain the drive for research, learn from our findings, and adopt, uphold, and carry with us the appropriate political and societal will.

Keywords Future challenges · Quality of life · Political will

Mine is not an argument to defund the police; it is not an argument to close prisons or to prohibit youth detention. It is, rather, an argument to spend our dollars and energies on strategies that are more likely to achieve the outcomes that we want.

© The Author(s), under exclusive license to Springer Nature Singapore Pte Ltd. 2024
R. Sarre, *Preventing Crime*,
https://doi.org/10.1007/978-981-97-3488-7_12

On February 12, 2024, The Advertiser (the daily newspaper) in Adelaide published a letter of mine which captures the essence of my quest to drive a different narrative around crime prevention and, in this instance, juvenile justice.

> Dear Sir/Madam,
> The incidence of repeated break-ins and shoplifting by teenagers ('Our shops plagued by crime spree' *The Advertiser* February 9) is worrisome and unacceptable. But equally unacceptable is a response that simply locks these kids away for months if not years. There is a truism in justice studies that the best predictor of a person's adult life in crime is the depth to which they are taken into the justice system as a juvenile. True, the alternative services that will rescue them, namely education, skills training, housing, care, mental health promotion, and mentoring are expensive. But given that half a billion dollars are spent each year on detaining kids aged 10-17 across Australia, there's plenty of money going around to be reinvested into these young and vulnerable lives as they transition into adulthood.
> Yours sincerely

This theme, namely that formal criminal justice processes need to take a back step if Australia is serious about preventing crime, has been the subject of similar letters of mine for decades, yet nothing changes.

I conclude with a statement that was made at the end of the Recommendations section of the remarkably prescient report of the National Committee on Violence thirty four years ago.

> Given the enormous financial burdens which current levels of violence impose on contemporary Australia ... Australian governments are faced with a stark choice – either to pay now, and make Australian society less violent; or to pay later, and suffer the costs amounting to hundreds of millions of dollars per year, and, in addition, cause Australians to endure the pronounced deterioration in the quality of life which the aftermath of violence imposes on our society. (National Committee on Violence, 1990, p. xlvii)

The authors' words were directed specifically at violence prevention. But they could equally apply to the directions needed for effective crime prevention more generally. Social justice policies (improving health, housing, education, employment, welfare, mentoring, mental well-being) are expensive, and their effectiveness may not be apparent for a generation or two. But these costs need to be borne today, otherwise the problems we face will still be with our grandchildren and beyond. Greater expenditures will be required in the long term if this message is not heeded, and we fail to act accordingly. Readers should not forget, too, that government budgets are all about setting priorities. If Australian policymakers can commit hundreds of billions of dollars on submarines and tax cuts, we can afford to spend a fraction of those dollars on social policies that will have a guaranteed long term crime reductive effect.

Also prescient are the words found at the conclusion of *The Honest Politicians' Guide to Crime Control*, where Morris and Hawkins reflect on the task that they maintained would address the failings and inadequacies of their target: the American justice system.

> It is perverse to pretend that we do not know how to deal with crime much more effectively than we do deal with it. Nor is it true that lack of money is the major obstacle to improving the operations of the criminal justice system. ... [Indeed] it is inertia far more than ignorance or inadequate resources which impedes action. ... The problem of crime like the problem of disease is not in any final sense soluble. But it can be subjected to effective control. We cannot expect more; there is no reason why we should be satisfied with less. (Morris and Hawkins, 1970, p. 262)

When it comes to crime abatement, we have clear choices. In the discussion above I have put my preferred choices. They are achievable if we have the appropriate political will, and if we take the long view. Taking that long view needs to start now.

References

ABS. (2019a). *Crime Victimisation 2018–2019, Australia*. Cat no 4530.0 Australian Bureau of Statistics. http://www.abs.gov.au/ausstats/abs@.nsf/mf/4530.0. Accessed January 6, 2022.

ABS. (2019b). *Prisoners in Australia*. Cat no 4517.0. Australian Bureau of Statistics. http://www.abs.gov.au/ausstats/abs@.nsf/mf/4517.0. Accessed January 6, 2022.

ABS. (2024). *Prisoners in Australia 2023*. Cat no 4517.0. Australian Bureau of Statistics. Prisoners in Australia, 2023 | Australian Bureau of Statistics (abs.gov.au). Accessed January 30, 2024.

AIHW. (2022). *Youth Justice in Australia 2020–2021*. Australian Institute of Health and Welfare. https://www.aihw.gov.au/getmedia/10da194d-5756-4933-be0a-29d41743d79b/aihw-juv-138.pdf.aspx?inline=true. Accessed January 6, 2022.

Alcohol and Drug Foundation. (2021). *Pill Testing*. https://adf.org.au/insights/pill-testing-australia/. Accessed January 6, 2022.

Almond, P. (2008). Public Perceptions of Work-Related Fatality Cases: Reaching the Outer Limits of 'Populist Punitiveness'? *British Journal of Criminology, 48*, 448–467.

Andrejevic, M. (2012). Brain Whisperers: Cutting Through the Clutter with Neuromarketing. *Somatechnics, 2*(2), 198–215.

Antolak-Saper, N. (2023). *The Role of the Media in Criminal Justice Policy: Prisons, Populism and the Press*. Routledge.

Australian Cyber Security Centre. (2017). *Australian Cyber Security Centre 2017 Threat Report*. https://www.acsc.gov.au/publications/ACSC_Threat_Report_2017.pdf. Accessed January 6, 2022.

© The Editor(s) (if applicable) and The Author(s), under exclusive license to Springer Nature Singapore Pte Ltd. 2024
R. Sarre, *Preventing Crime*,
https://doi.org/10.1007/978-981-97-3488-7

Australian Government. (2013). *Value of a Justice Reinvestment Approach to Criminal Justice in Australia*. Senate Legal and Constitutional Affairs Committee, Parliament House, Canberra.

Australian Government. (2015). *The Ability of Australian Law Enforcement Authorities to Eliminate Gun-related Violence in the Community*. Senate Legal and Constitutional Affairs References Committee, Parliament House, Canberra. http://www.aph.gov.au/Parliamentary_Business/Committees/Senate/Legal_and_Constitutional_Affairs/Illicit_firearms/Report. Accessed January 6, 2022.

Australian Government. (2023a). *Response to the Parliamentary Joint Committee on Intelligence and Security Report: Review of the Mandatory Data Retention Regime*. Parliament House, Canberra.

Australian Government. (2023b). *The National Plan to End Violence Against Women and Children 2022–2032: Ending Gender-based Violence in One Generation*. Parliament House, Canberra.

Australian Human Rights Commission. (2021). *Press Release*. https://humanrights.gov.au/about/news/media-releases/australians-deserve-tech-protects-their-rights. Accessed February 1, 2023.

Australian Human Rights Commission. (2022). *Independent Review into Commonwealth Parliamentary Workplaces*. https://humanrights.gov.au/CPWReview. Accessed February 2, 2024.

Australian Parliament. (2017). *Review of the Implementation Period of the Telecommunications (Interception and Access) Amendment (Data Retention) Act 2014*. Joint Parliamentary Committee on Intelligence and Security, Parliament House, Canberra.

Ayling, J. (2013). Haste Makes Waste: Deliberative Improvements for Serious Crime Legislation. *Australian and New Zealand Journal of Criminology, 46*(1), 12–31.

Bacchi, C. (2012). Introducing the 'What's the Problem Represented to be' Approach. In A. Bletsas & C. Beasley (Eds.), *Engaging with Carol Bacchi: Strategic Interventions and Exchanges* (pp. 21–24). University of Adelaide Press.

Bailey, J., Henry, N., & Flynn, A. (2021). Technology-Facilitated Violence and Abuse: International Perspectives and Experiences. In J. Bailey & A. Flynn (Eds.), *The Emerald International Handbook of Technology-Facilitated Violence and Abuse* (pp. 1–17). Emerald Publishing.

Baker, D. (2013). *Tough on Crime: The Rhetoric and Reality of Property Crime and Feeling Safe in Australia* (Policy Brief, no. 56). Manuka, ACT: The Australia Institute.

Baldry, E. (2014). Complex Needs and the Justice System. In C. Chamberlain, G. Johnson, & C. Robinson (Eds.), *Homelessness in Australia: An Introduction*. UNSW Press.

Bangalore, S., & Messerli, F. H. (2013). Gun Ownership and Firearm-related Deaths. *The American Journal of Medicine, 126*(10), 873–876.

Barkworth, J., & Murphy, K. (2015). Procedural Justice Policing and Citizen Compliance Behaviour: The Importance of Emotion. *Psychology, Crime and Law, 2*(3), 254–273.

Barratt, M. J., Hughes, C. E., Ferris, J. A., & Winstock, A. R. (2019). *Australian Music Festival Attendees Who Seek Emergency Medical Treatment Following Alcohol and Other Drug Use: A Global Drug Survey Data Report*. RMIT University.

Bartkowiak-Théron, I., & Asquith, N. (2016). Conceptual Divides and Practice Synergies in Law Enforcement and Public Health: Some Lessons from Policing Vulnerability in Australia. *Policing and Society, 27*, 276–288.

Bauer, S. (2018). *American Prison: A Reporter's Undercover Journey into the Business of Punishment*. Penguin.

Bayley, D. (1993). Back from Wonderland, or Toward the Rational Use of Police Resources. In A. N. Doob (Ed.), *Thinking About Police Resources, Research Report no. 26* (pp. 1–34). Centre of Criminology.

Bayley, D. (1994). It's Accountability Stupid! In K. Bryett & C. Lewis (Eds.), *Unpeeling Tradition: Contemporary Policing* (pp. 124–140). CAPSM.

Bell, C., & Coates, D. (2022). *The Effectiveness of Interventions for Perpetrators of Domestic and Family Violence: An Overview of Findings from Reviews*. ANROWS.

Bennett, P. (2015). *Specialist Courts for Sentencing Aboriginal Offenders: Aboriginal Courts in Australia*. Federation Press.

Blumenfeld, S., Anderson, G., & Hooper, V. (2020). Covid-19 and Employee Surveillance. *New Zealand Journal of Employment Relations, 45*(2), 42–56.

Boffa, J., Tilton, E., & Ah Chee, D. (2018). Preventing Alcohol-related Harm in Aboriginal and Torres Strait Islander Communities: The Experience of an Aboriginal Community Controlled Health Service in Central Australia. *Australian Journal of General Practice, 47*(12), 851–854.

Braithwaite, J. (1996). Restorative Justice and a Better Future. *The Dalhousie Review, 76*(1), 9–32.

Braithwaite, J. (2022). *Macrocriminology and Freedom*. ANU Press.

Brantingham, P., & Brantingham, P. (2008). Crime Pattern Theory. In R. Wortley & L. Mazerolle (Eds.), *Environmental Criminology and Crime Analysis* (pp. 78–94). Willan.

Brewer, R., de Vel-Palumbo, M., Hutchings, A., Holt, T., Goldsmith, A., & Maimon, D. (2019). *Cybercrime Prevention: Theory and Applications*. Palgrave Macmillan.

Bright, D., Halsey, M., Goldsmith, A., & Goudie, S. (2023). "I Know a Guy and He's Got Guns Galore": Accessing Crime Guns in the Australian Illicit Firearms Market. *Deviant Behavior, 44*(5), 671–689.

Broadhurst, R. (2002). Crime and Indigenous People. In A. Graycar & P. Grabosky (Eds.), *The Cambridge Handbook of Australian Criminology*. Cambridge University Press.

Broadhurst, R. (2017). Cybercrime. In A. Deckert & R. Sarre (Eds.), *The Palgrave Handbook of Australian and New Zealand Criminology, Crime and Justice* (pp. 221–236). Palgrave Macmillan.

Bullock, K., & Tilley, N. (2009). Problem-Oriented Policing. In A. Wakefield & J. Fleming (Eds.), *The Sage Dictionary of Policing* (pp. 245–248). Sage.

Burdekin, B. (2014). *Private Correspondence*. Speech to the University of South Australia law degree graduation ceremony, Adelaide, South Australia, 20 August, 2014.

Button, M. (2008). *Doing Security*. Palgrave Macmillan.

Canny, G. (2022). *Why Raising the Age Makes Sense*. Legal Services Commission of SA. https://lsc.sa.gov.au/cb_pages/news/Whyraisingtheagemakessense.php#:~:text=Inpercent20SApercent20atpercent20thepercent20present,bepercent20overturnedpercent20forpercent20seriouspercent20crimes. Accessed January 6, 2022.

Carriere, K., & Ericson, R. (1989). *Crime Stoppers: A Study in the Organization of Community Policing*. Research Report. Centre of Criminology, University of Toronto.

Catanzariti, J. (2004, August). Higher and Novel Penalties for Serious Safety Breaches. *Law Society Journal, 42*(7), 48.

Center on Juvenile and Criminal Justice. (2019). *High Rates of Incarceration Not Linked to Less Crime*. https://www.cjcj.org/news/blog/high-rates-of-incarceration-not-linked-to-less-crime. Accessed February 1, 2024.

Chang, L. Y. C., Zhong, L. Y., & Grabosky, P. N. (2018). Citizen co-Production of Cyber Security: Self-help, Vigilantes, and Cybercrime. *Regulation and Governance, 12*(1), 101–114.

Chapman, S. (1998). *Over Our Dead Bodies: Port Arthur and Australia's Fight for Gun Control*. Pluto Press.

Chappell, D. (2014). Firearms Regulation, Violence and the Mentally Ill: A Contemporary Antipodean Appraisal. *International Journal of Law and Psychiatry, 37*, 399–408.

Chappell, D. (2016). Shooting, Spanking, Punching and Other Matters: Reflections on the Work and Impact of the National Committee on Violence. In J. Stubbs & S. Tomsen (Eds.), *Australian Violence: Crime, Criminal Justice and Beyond* (pp. 14–30). Federation Press.

Cherney, A. (2000). The Adoption of "What Works" Principles in Crime Prevention Policy and Practice. *Current Issues in Criminal Justice, 12*(1), 93–97.

Clancey, G. (2020). Teaching Crime Prevention and Community Safety. In D. Palmer (Ed.), *Scholarship of Teaching and Learning in Criminology* (pp. 59–85). Palgrave Macmillan.

Clancey, G., Fisher, D., & Yeung, N. (2016). A Recent History of Australian Crime Prevention. *Crime Prevention and Community Safety, 18*, 309–328.

Clancey, G., & Lin, B. (2021). Crime Prevention and Reduction. In D. Palmer, W. de Lint, & D. Dalton (Eds.), *Crime and Justice: A Guide to Criminology* (6th ed., pp. 475–495). Thomson Reuters.

Clancey, G., & Metcalfe, L. (2020). A Review of Crime Prevention Activities in an Australian Local Government Area Since the Late 1980s. *Crime Prevention and Community Safety, 22*, 49–67.

Clancey, G., Monchuk, L., Anderson, J., & Ellis, J. (2018). Lost in Implementation: NSW Police for Crime Prevention Officer Perspectives on Crime Prevention Through Environmental Design. *Crime Prevention and Community Safety, 20*, 139–153.

Clarke, R. V., & Felson, M. (Eds). (1993). *Routine Activity and Rational Choice: Advances in Criminological Theory 5*. Transaction Publishers.

Clear, T., & Frost, N. (2014). *The Punishment Imperative: The Rise and Failure of Mass Incarceration in America*. New York University Press.

Clough, J. (2005). Will the Punishment Fit the Crime? Corporate Manslaughter and the Problem of Sanction. *Flinders Journal of Law Reform, 8*(1), 113–131.

College of Policing. (2013). *What Works*. Centre for Crime Reduction. http://whatworks.college.police.uk/toolkit/Pages/Toolkit.aspx. Accessed October 20, 2023.

Cornish, D. B., & Clarke, R. V. (2008). The Rational Choice Perspective. In R. Wortley & L. Mazerolle (Eds.), *Environmental Criminology and Crime Analysis* (pp. 21–47). Willan.

Crime and Corruption Commission. (2018). *Taskforce Flaxton: An Examination of Corruption Risks and Corruption in Queensland Prisons*. Crime and Corruption Commission.

Cunneen, C. (2001). *Conflict, Politics and Crime: Aboriginal Communities and the Police*. Allen & Unwin.

Cunneen, C., & Rowe, S. (2014). Changing Narratives: Colonised Peoples, Criminology and Social Work. *International Journal for Crime, Justice and Social Democracy, 3*(1), 49–67.

Currie, E. (1998). *Crime and Punishment in America: Why the Solutions to America's Most Stubborn Social Crisis Have Not Worked—And What Will*. Metropolitan Books.

Currie, E. (2008). *The Roots of Danger: Violent Crime in Global Perspective*. Prentice Hall.

Currie, E. (2013). Consciousness, Solidarity and Hope as Prevention and Rehabilitation. *International Journal for Crime, Justice and Social Democracy, 2*, 3–11.
Daly, K. (2014). *Redressing Institutional Abuse of Children*. Palgrave Macmillan.
Davidson, P., Bradbury, B., Wong, M., & Hill, T. (2023). *Inequality in Australia 2023: Overview*. Australian Council of Social Service and the University of New South Wales, Sydney.
de Waard, J. (2022). *What Works? A Systematic Overview of Published Meta Evaluations/Synthesis Studies Within the Knowledge Domains of Situational Crime Prevention, Policing, and Criminal Justice Interventions, 1997–2022*. Dutch Ministry of Justice and Security, Law Enforcement Department, Unit for General Crime Policy.
Dearne, K. (2001, May 1). Prescribing a Privacy Cure. *The Australian IT*.
Deckert, A. (2016). Criminologists, Duct Tape, and Indigenous People: Quantifying the Use of Silencing Research Methods. *International Journal of Comparative and Applied Criminal Justice, 40*(1), 43–62.
Deckert, A., & Sarre, R. (Eds.). (2017). *The Palgrave Handbook of Australian and New Zealand Criminology, Crime and Justice*. Palgrave Macmillan.
Developmental Crime Prevention Consortium. (1999). *Pathways to Prevention: Developmental and Early Intervention Approaches to Crime in Australia*. http://eprints.qut.edu.au/4482/1/4482_report.pdf. Accessed January 6, 2022.
Dixon, D. (2005). Why Don't the Police Stop Crime? *The Australian and New Zealand Journal of Criminology, 8*(1), 4–24.
Donnelly, N., Menendez, P., & Mahoney, N. (2015). *The Effect of Liquor Licence Concentrations in Local Areas on Rates of Assault in New South Wales*. NSW Bureau of Crime Statistics and Research.
Draper, R., Ritchie, J., & Prenzler, T. (2012). Making the Most of Security Technology. In T. Prenzler (Ed.), *Policing and Security in Practice: Challenges and Achievements* (pp. 186–203). Palgrave Macmillan.
Dreisinger, B. (2016). *Incarceration Nations: A Journey to Justice in Prisons Around the World*. Random House.
Durlauf, S., & Nagin, D. (2011). Imprisonment and Crime: Can Both be Reduced? *Criminology and Public Policy, 11*(1), 9–54.
Eriksson, L., Mazerolle, P., & McPhedran, S. (2022). *Giving Voice to the Silenced Victims: A Qualitative Study of Intimate Partner Femicide* (Trends and Issues in Crime and criminal Justice no. 645). Australian Institute of Criminology.
Farrell, G. (2013). Five Tests for a Theory of the Crime Drop. *Crime Science, 2*(5), 1–8.
Farrell, G., Tilley, N., & Tseloni, A. (2014). Why the Crime Drop? *Crime and Justice, 43*(1), 421–490.

Fasman, J. (2021). *We See It All: Liberty and Justice in an Age of Perpetual Surveillance*. Scribe.

Fergusson, D., Boden, J., & Horwood, L. J. (2015). From Evidence to Policy: Findings from the Christchurch Health and Development Study. *Australian and New Zealand Journal of Criminology, 48*(3), 386–408.

Finland. (2020). *NUMBEO*. https://www.numbeo.com/crime/country_result.jsp?country=Finland. Accessed February 1, 2023.

Fitz-Gibbon, K., Walklate, S., McCulloch, J., & Maher, J. M. (2023). Intimate Femicide/Intimate Partner Femicide. In M. Dawson & S. Mobayed Vega (Eds.), *The Routledge International Handbook on Femicide and Feminicide* (pp. 301–310). Routledge.

Flannery, A. (2019). *Next Regulatory Steps Taken for Australia's Consumer Data Right*. https://www.holdingredlich.com/next-regulatory-steps-taken-for-australia-s-consumer-data-right. Accessed February 1, 2023.

Fleming, J., & Wood, J. (Eds.). (2006). *Fighting Crime Together: The Challenges of Policing and Security Networks*. UNSW Press.

Freiberg, A. (2003). Therapeutic Jurisprudence in Australia: Paradigm Shift or Pragmatic Incrementalism? *Law in Context, 20*(2), 6–23.

Gant, F., & Grabosky, P. (2000). *The Promise of Crime Prevention* (2nd ed.). Research and Public Policy Series, no. 31. Australian Institute of Criminology.

Gelb, K. (2011). *Predictors of Confidence: Community Views in Victoria*. Sentencing Advisory Council.

Gendreau, P., & Ross, R. R. (1987). Revivification of Rehabilitation: Evidence from the 1980s. *Justice Quarterly, 4*(3), 349–407.

Gill, M. (2006). CCTV: Is it Effective? In M. Gill (Ed.), *Handbook of Security* (1st ed., 438–461). Palgrave Macmillan.

Gill, M. (2013). Engaging the Corporate Sector in Policing: Realities and Opportunities. *Policing, 7*(3), 273–279.

Gobert, J., & Punch, M. (2003). *Rethinking Corporate Crime*. LexisNexis Butterworths.

Goldsmith, A., & Wall, D. (2022). The Seductions of Cybercrime: Adolescence and the Thrills of Digital Transgression. *European Journal of Criminology, 19*(1), 98–117.

Goldstein, H. (1979). *Problem-Oriented Policing*. McGraw-Hill.

Gordon, S., & Ford, R. (2006). On the Definition and Classification of Cybercrime. *Journal of Computer Virology, 2*, 13–20.

Grabosky, P. (1992). Law Enforcement and the Citizen: Non-Governmental Participants in Crime Prevention and Control. *Policing and Society, 2*, 249–271.

Grabosky, P. (1995). Using Non-Governmental Resources to Foster Regulatory Compliance, *Governance: An International Journal of Policy and Administration, 8*(4), 527–550.

Grabosky, P. (2007). *Electronic Crime*. Prentice Hall.
Grabosky, P. (2012). The Campbell Collaboration Crime and Justice Group. In R. Thilagaraj, J. Liu, & S. Latha (Eds.), *Crime and Criminal Justice in Asia* (pp. 25–30). Mittal Publications.
Grabosky, P. (2023). Foreword. In R. Smith, R. Sarre, L. Chang, & L. Lau (Eds.), *Cybercrime in the Pandemic Digital Age and Beyond*. Palgrave Macmillan.
Gramlich, J. (2022). *What the Data Says About Gun Deaths in the USA*. Pew Research Center. https://www.pewresearch.org/fact-tank/2022/02/03/what-the-data-says-about-gun-deaths-in-the-u-s/. Accessed February 1, 2023.
Hällsten, M., Szulkin, R., & Sarnecki, J. (2013). Crime as a Price of Inequality? The Gap in Registered Crime Between Childhood Immigrants, Children of Immigrants and Children of Native Swedes. *British Journal of Criminology, 53*(3), 456–481.
Halsey, M., & Deegan, S. (2015). *Young Offenders: Crime, Prison and Struggles for Desistance*. Palgrave Studies in Prisons and Penology. Palgrave Macmillan.
Harding, R. (1997). *Private Prisons and Public Accountability*. Open University Press.
Harding, R. (2003). Influencing Policy: Successes and Failures of Criminological Research in Australia. In L. Zedner & A. Ashworth (Eds.), *The Criminological Foundations of Penal Policy: Essays in Honour of Roger Hood* (pp. 463–483). Oxford University Press.
Harvard. (2002). *Homicide*. Harvard School of Public Health. http://www.hsph.harvard.edu/hicrc/firearms-research/guns-and-death/. Accessed February 1, 2024.
Haslam, D., Mathews, B., Pacella, R., Scott, J. G., Finkelhor, D., Higgins, D. J., Meinck, F., Erskine, H. E., Thomas, H. J., Lawrence, D., & Malacova, E. (2023). *The Prevalence and Impact of Child Maltreatment in Australia: Findings from the Australian Child Maltreatment Study: Brief Report*. Queensland University of Technology.
Head, B., Ferguson, M., Cherney, A., & Boreham, P. (2014). Are Policymakers Interested in Social Research? Exploring the Sources and Uses of Valued Information Among Public Servants in Australia. *Policy and Society, 33*, 89–101.
Heseltine, K., Day, A., & Sarre, R. (2011). *Prison-Based Correctional Offender Rehabilitation Programs: The 2009 National Picture in Australia* (Research and Public Policy Series, no. 112). Australian Institute of Criminology.
Hill, J. (2002). Corporate Criminal Liability in Australia: An Evolving Corporate Governance Technique? In C. K. Low (Ed.), *Corporate Governance: An Asia-Pacific Critique* (p. 519). Sweet and Maxwell.

Homel, P. (2004). *The Whole of Government Approach to Crime Prevention.* (Trends and Issues in Crime and Criminal Justice, no. 287). Australian Institute of Criminology.

Homel, P., & Fuller, G. (2015). *Understanding the Local Government Role in Crime Prevention* (Trends and Issues in Crime and Criminal Justice no. 505). Australian Institute of Criminology.

Homel, R. J. (2021). Developmental Crime Prevention in the Twenty-first Century: Generating Better Evidence Embedded in Large-scale Delivery Systems. *Journal of Developmental and Life-Course Criminology, 7*(1), 112–125.

Homel, R. J., & Freiberg, K. (2017). Developmental Prevention. In A. Deckert & R. Sarre (Eds.), *The Palgrave Handbook of Australian and New Zealand Criminology, Crime and Justice* (pp. 815–830). Palgrave Macmillan.

Homel, R. J., Freiberg, K., & Branch, S. (2015). CREATE-ing Capacity to Take Developmental Crime Prevention to Scale: A Community-based Approach Within a National Framework. *Australian and New Zealand Journal of Criminology, 48*(3), 367–385.

Homel, R. J., & McGee, T. (2012). Community Approaches to Crime and Violence Prevention: Building Prevention Capacity. In R. Loeber & B. Welsh (Eds.), *The Future of Criminology* (pp. 172–177). Oxford University Press.

Hora, P. (2010). *Smart Justice: Building Safer Communities, Increasing Access to the Courts, and Elevating Trust and Confidence in the Justice System.* Department of Premier and Cabinet, Government of South Australia.

Hough, M., Jackson, J., & Bradford, B. (2013). Legitimacy, Trust and Compliance: An Empirical Test of Procedural Justice Theory Using the European Social Survey. In J. Tankebe & A. Liebling (Eds.), *Legitimacy and Criminal Justice: An International Exploration* (pp. 326–352). Oxford University Press.

Howells, K., Heseltine, K., Sarre, R., Davey, L., & Day, A. (2004). *Correctional Offender Rehabilitation Programs: The National Picture in Australia.* Report to the Criminology Research Council. http://www.criminologyresearchcouncil.gov.au/reports/200405-03.pdf. Accessed February 1, 2023.

Hughes, C. E., Chalmers, J., & Bright, D. A. (2020). Exploring Interrelationships Between High-level Drug Trafficking and Other Serious and Organised Crime: An Australian Study. *Global Crime, 21*(1), 28–50.

Hughes, C. E., Seear, K., Ritter, A., & Mazerolle, L. (2019). *Criminal Justice Responses Relating to Personal Use and Possession of Illicit Drugs: The Reach of Australian Drug Diversion Programs and Barriers and Facilitators to Expansion* (Drug Policy Modelling Program, Monograph no. 27). National Drug and Alcohol Research Centre, UNSW.

Johnson, S. D., Tilley, N., & Bowers, K. J. (2015). Introducing EMMIE: An Evidence Rating Scale to Encourage Mixed-method Crime Prevention Synthesis Reviews. *Journal of Experimental Criminology, 11*, 459–473.

Justice Reform Initiative. (2020). *The State of The Incarceration Nation: A Briefing To Australia's Members of Parliament*. Justice Reform Initiative. https://www.justicereforminitiative.org.au/reports. Accessed October 2, 2023.

Kelly, M., & Tubex, H. (2015). Stemming the Tide of Aboriginal Incarceration. *The University of Notre Dame Australia Law Review, 17*, 1–17.

Klockars, C. (1981). *Thinking About Police*. The Police Foundation.

Korff, J. (2022). *Prison Rates: Creative Spirits*. https://www.creativespirits.info/aboriginalculture/law/aboriginal-prison-rates. Accessed January 6, 2022.

Kowalick, P., Connery, D., & Sarre, R. (2018). Intelligence-sharing in the Context of Policing Transnational Serious and Organized Crime: A Note on Policy and Practice in an Australian Setting. *Police Practice and Research: An International Journal, 19*(6), 596–608.

Lab, S. P. (2023). *Crime Prevention: Approaches, Practices, and Evaluations* (11th ed.). Routledge.

Laycock, G. (2014). Crime Science and Policing: Lessons of Translation. *Policing, 8*(4), 393–401.

Lee, N. (2017, February 14). "Ice Wars" Message Is Overblown and Unhelpful. *The Conversation*. https://theconversation.com/ice-wars-message-is-overblown-and-unhelpful Accessed February 1, 2023.

Lee, W., & Suardi, S. (2008). *The Australian Firearms Buyback and Its Effect on Gun Deaths* (Melbourne Institute Working Paper Series, no. 17). Melbourne Institute.

Leigh, A. (2019). *Mass Imprisonment Returns: Estimating and Explaining Long-Run Incarceration Rates for Australia and Comparator Nations* (Unpublished paper). Parliament House.

Lemieux, F. (2024). Mass Shootings in the United States. *Oxford Research Encyclopedia of Criminology and Criminal Justice*, forthcoming.

Lemieux, F., Bricknell, S., & Prenzler, T. (2015). Mass Shootings in Australia and the United States, 1981–2013. *Journal of Criminological Research, Policy and Practice, 1*(3), 131–142.

Lester, D. (1990). The Relationship Between Firearm Availability and Primary and Secondary Murder. *Psychological Reports, 67*(2), 490.

Leymon, M., Campbell, C., Henning, K., & Renauer, B. (2022). The Impacts of Length of Prison Stay on Recidivism of Non-Violent Offenders. *Journal of Criminal Justice, 82*, 1–12.

Lipton, D. S. (1998, August). *The Effectiveness of Correctional Treatment Revisited Thirty Years Later: Preliminary Meta-Analytic Findings from the CDATE Study* (Unpublished paper presented to the 12th International Congress on Criminology). Seoul Korea.

Lipton, D. S., Martinson, R., & Wilks, J. (1975). *The Effectiveness of Correctional Treatment: A Survey of Treatment Valuation Studies*. Praeger Press.

Livings, B. (2021). What Do Judges Mean When They Sentence to Protect the Safety of the Community? *Current Issues in Criminal Justice, 33*(2), 247–263.
Livings, B., & Sarre, R. (2023). Roman Tomasic's Rejection of a Poor Corporate Culture as a Tool for Tackling Corporate Malfeasance: A Reflection and Rejoinder. *Australian Journal of Corporate Law, 38*, 348–361.
Livingston, M. (2011). A Longitudinal Analysis of Alcohol Outlet Density and Domestic Violence. *Addiction, 106*(5), 919–925.
Malvaso, C., Day, A., McLachlan, K., Sarre, R., Lynch, J., & Pilkington, R. (2024). Welfare, Justice, Child Development and Human Rights: A Review of the Objects of Youth Justice Legislation in Australia. *Current Issues in Criminal Justice.* https://doi.org/10.1080/10345329.2024.2313784.
Marchetti, E. (2014). Delivering Justice in Indigenous Sentencing Courts: What this Means for Judicial Officers, Elders, Community Representatives and Indigenous Court Workers. *Law & Policy, 36*(4), 341–369.
Marchetti, E. (2015). An Australian Indigenous-Focused Justice Response to Intimate Partner Violence: Offenders' Perceptions of the Sentencing Process. *British Journal of Criminology, 55*(1), 88–106.
Marmo, M., & Chazal, N. (2010). The Trafficked Woman: Ideal or Blameworthy Victim? *Advances in Sociology Research, 17*, 125–140.
Marshall, C. D. (2015). A Gracious Legacy: Changing Lenses in New Zealand. *International Journal of Restorative Justice, 3*(3), 439–444.
Marshall, C. D. (2020). Restorative Justice. In P. Babie & R. Sarre (Eds.), *Religion Matters: The Contemporary Relevance of Religion* (pp. 101–118). Springer.
Martinson, R. (1974). What Works? Questions and Answers About Prison Reform. *The Public Interest, 35*, 22–54.
Mathews, B., Papalia, N., Napier, S., Malacova, E., Lawrence, D., Higgins, D. J., Thomas, H., Erskine, H., Meinck, F., Haslam, D., Scott, J. G., Finkelhor, D., & Pacella, R. (2023). *Child Maltreatment and Criminal Justice System Involvement in Australia: Findings from a National Survey* (Trends and Issues in Crime and Criminal Justice, no. 681). Australian Institute of Criminology.
Mazerolle, L., Bennett, S., Antrobus, E., Eggins, E., & Martin, P. (2015). Enhancing Police legitimacy: Results from the Queensland Community Engagement Trial (QCET). *Australian Institute of Police Management, Research Focus, 3*(4), 1–8.
McCausland, R., & Baldry, E. (2023, April 17). The Social Determinants of Justice: Eight Factors that Increase Your Risk of imprisonment. *The Conversation.* https://theconversation.com/the-social-determinants-of-justice-8-factors-that-increase-your-risk-of-imprisonment-203661. Accessed January 30, 2024.

McCold, P. (2001). Primary Restorative Justice Practices. In A. Morris & G. Maxwell (Eds.), *Restorative Justice for Juveniles: Conferencing, Mediation and Circles* (pp. 41–58). Hart Publishing.

McGee, T., & Mazerolle, P. (Eds.). (2015). *Developmental and Life-Course Theories of Crime*. Ashgate.

McGuire, M., & Dowling, S. (2013). *Cybercrime: A Review of the Evidence: Summary of Key Findings and Implications* (Home Office Research Report no. 75). Home Office.

McLachlan, K. J. (2023). 'Raising the Age' of Criminal Responsibility Is a Key Strategy in Providing Trauma-Informed Responses to Children. *Current Issues in Criminal Justice*. https://doi.org/10.1007/10.1080/10345329.2023.2196099

Millard, C. (2012). Communications Privacy. In I. Walden (Ed.), *Telecommunications Law* (4th ed.). Oxford University Press.

Morris, N., & Hawkins, G. (1970). *The Honest Politicians' Guide to Crime Control*. University of Chicago Press.

Moss, K., & Stephens, M. (Eds.). (2006). *Crime Reduction and the Law*. Routledge.

Moulds, S., & Krishna, K. (2020). Old Enough to Know Better? Reform Options for South Australia's Age of Criminality Laws. *The Adelaide Law Review*, *41*(1), 313–323.

Murphy, K., & Barkworth, J. (2014). Victim Willingness to Report Crime to Police: Does Procedural Justice or Outcome Matter Most? *Victims and Offenders*, *9*(2), 178–204.

National Committee on Violence. (1990). *Violence: Directions for Australia*. Australian Institute of Criminology.

NSW Department of Communities and Justice. (2023). *Aboriginal-led Early Support Programs for Aboriginal Children, Young People, Families, and Communities: A Review of the Evidence Base*. Gamarada.

Norden, P. (2021). *Seeking Justice in the Criminal Justice System in Australia*. Norden Directions.

O'Donnell, J. (2022). *Mapping Social Cohesion*. Scanlon Foundation Research Institute.

Olds, D. (2008). Preventing Child Maltreatment and Crime with Prenatal and Infancy Support of Parents: The Nurse-Family Partnership. *Journal of Scandinavian Studies in Criminology and Crime Prevention*, *9*(1), 2–24.

Olds, D., Kitzman, H., Knudtson, M., Anson, E., Smith, J., & Cole, R. (2014). Effect of Home Visiting by Nurses on Maternal and Child Mortality: Results of a Two-Decade Follow-up of a Randomized Clinical Trial. *JAMA Pediatrics*, *168*(9), 800–806.

Oleson, J. (2017). Sentencing Theories, Practices, and Trends. In A. Deckert & R. Sarre (Eds.), *The Australian and New Zealand Handbook of Criminology, Crime and Justice* (pp. 363–378). Palgrave Macmillan.

Payne, J., & Gaffney, A. (2012). *How Much Crime Is Drug or Alcohol Related? Self-reported Attributions of Police Detainees* (Trends and Issues in Crime and Criminal Justice no. 439). Australian Institute of Criminology.

Petersen, D. S., & Das, D. (Eds.). (2018). *Global Perspectives on Crime Prevention and Community Resilience*. Routledge.

Piquero, A., Jennings, W., Farrington, D. P., Diamond, B., & Reingle Gonzalez, J. M. (2016). A Meta-analysis Update on the Effectiveness of Early Self-control Improvement Programs to Improve Self-control and Reduce Delinquency. *Journal of Experimental Criminology, 12*(2), 249–264.

Prenzler, T. (2011). Strike Force Piccadilly and ATM Security: A Follow-up Study. *Policing, 5*(3), 236–247.

Prenzler, T. (Ed.). (2017). *Understanding Crime Prevention: The Case Study Approach*. Australian Academic Press.

Prenzler, T., & Sarre, R. (2002). The Policing Complex. In A. Graycar & P. Grabosky (Eds.), *The Cambridge Handbook of Australian Criminology* (pp. 52–72). Cambridge University Press.

Prenzler, T., & Sarre, R. (2008a). Developing a Risk Profile and Model Regulatory System for the Security Industry. *Security Journal, 21,* 264–277.

Prenzler, T., & Sarre, R. (2008b). Protective Security in Australia: Scandal, Media Images and Reform. *Journal of Policing, Intelligence and Counter Terrorism, 3*(2), 23–37.

Prenzler, T., & Sarre, R. (2012). Public-Private Crime Prevention Partnerships. In T. Prenzler (Ed.), *Policing and Security in Practice: Challenges and Achievements* (pp. 149–167). Palgrave Macmillan.

Prenzler, T., & Sarre, R. (2014a). The Role of Partnerships in Security Management. In M. Gill (Ed.), *Handbook of Security* (2nd ed., pp. 769–790). Palgrave Macmillan.

Prenzler, T., & Sarre, R. (2014b). Smart Regulation for the Security Industry. In T. Prenzler (Ed.), *Professional Practice in Crime Prevention and Security Management* (pp. 175–191). Australian Academic Press.

Prenzler, T., & Sarre, R. (2017) The Security Industry and Crime Prevention. In T. Prenzler (Ed.), *Understanding Crime Prevention: The Case Study Approach* (pp. 167–183). Australian Academic Press.

Prenzler, T., & Sarre, R. (2021). Community Safety, Crime Prevention and 21st Century Policing. In P. Birch, M. Kennedy, & E. Kruger (Eds.), *Australian Policing: Critical Issues in 21st Century Police Practice* (pp. 283–298). Routledge.

Prenzler, T., & Sarre, R. (2022). Facilitating Best Practice in Security: The Role of Regulation. In M. Gill (Ed.), *Handbook of Security* (3rd ed., pp. 777–799). Palgrave Macmillan.

Prison Studies. (2020). https://www.prisonstudies.org/country/finland. Accessed February 1, 2023.

Productivity Commission. (2018). *New Australian Government Data Sharing and Release Legislation*. Australian Government. https://www.pc.gov.au/inquiries/completed/data-access#report. Accessed February 1, 2024.

Productivity Commission. (2021). *Australia's Prison Dilemma (An Investigation into Australia's Prison System)*. https://www.pc.gov.au/research/completed/prison-dilemma. Accessed February 1, 2024.

Productivity Commission. (2024a). *Report on Government Services: Police Services*. Australian Government. https://www.pc.gov.au/ongoing/report-on-government-services/2024/justice/police-services. Accessed February 1, 2024.

Productivity Commission. (2024b). *Report on Government Services: Corrective Services*. Australian Government. https://www.pc.gov.au/ongoing/report-on-government-services/2024/justice/corrective-services. Accessed February 1, 2024.

Productivity Commission. (2024c). *Report on Government Services: Justice*. Canberra: Australian Government, C Justice - Report on Government Services 2024-Productivity Commission. (https://www.pc.gov.au/ongoing/report-on-government-services/2024/justice/police-services). Accessed May 1, 2024.

Putnam, R. (2001). *Bowling Alone: The Collapse and Revival of American Community*. Simon & Schuster.

Putt, J., & Sarre, R. (2018). Policing in Remote Australia: Is It Possible to Ignore Colonial Borderlines? In D. Peterson & D. Das (Eds.), *Global Perspectives on Crime Prevention and Community Resilience* (pp. 119–132). CRC Press.

Queensland Audit Office. (2016). *Management of Privately Operated Prisons*. Queensland Government.

Ransley, J., & Mazerolle, L. (2017). Third Sector Involvement in Criminal Justice. In A. Deckert & R. Sarre (Eds.), *The Palgrave Handbook of Australian and New Zealand Criminology, Crime and Justice* (pp. 483–496). Palgrave Macmillan.

Ratcliffe, J. (2008). Intelligence-led Policing. In R. Wortley & L. Mazerolle (Eds.), *Environmental Criminology and Crime Analysis* (pp. 263–282). Willan.

Reiman, J. (2007). *The Rich Get Richer, and the Poor Get Prison*. Pearson.

Richards, K. (2009). Rewriting and Reclaiming History: An Analysis of the Emergence of Restorative Justice in Western Criminal Justice Systems. *The International Journal of Restorative Justice, 5*(1), 104–128.

Ritchie, D. (2012). *How Much Does Imprisonment Protect the Community Through Incapacitation?* Sentencing Advisory Council. Government of Victoria.

Ritter, A. (2022). *Drug Policy*. Routledge.

Royal Commission. (1991). *National Report of the Royal Commission into Aboriginal Deaths in Custody*, Vol. 3 (Commissioner Elliott Johnston QC). Australian Government Publishing Service.

Ruoti, S. (2022, April 7). How QR Codes Work and What Makes Them Dangerous—A Computer Scientist Explains. *The Conversation*. https://the conversation.com/how-qr-codes-work-and-what-makes-them-dangerous-a-computer-scientist-explains-177217. Accessed February 1, 2023.

Salter, M., Woodlock, D., & Dubler, N. (2023). Secrecy, Control and Violence in Women's Intimate Relationships with Child Sexual Abuse Material Offenders. In R. Brown (Ed.), *Crime and Justice Research 2023* (pp. 162–176). Australian Institute of Criminology.

SAPOL. (2021). *Annual Report 2020*. South Australia Police. Government Printer.

Sargeant, E., Murphy, K., Davis, J., & Mazerolle, L. (2012). Legitimacy and Policing. In T. Prenzler (Ed.), *Policing and Security in Practice: Challenges and Achievements* (pp. 20–36). Palgrave Macmillan.

Sarre, R. (1990). A Review of the Cannabis Expiation Notice Scheme in South Australia. *Australian and New Zealand Journal of Criminology, 23*, 299–303.

Sarre, R. (1991). Political Pragmatism Versus Informed Policy: Issues in the Design, Implementation and Evaluation of Anti-Violence Research and Programs. In D. Chappell, P. Grabosky, & H. Strang (Eds.), *Australian Violence: Contemporary Perspectives* (pp. 263–285). Australian Institute of Criminology.

Sarre, R. (1994). The Evaluation of Criminal Justice Initiatives: Some Observations on Models. *The Journal of Law and Information Science, 5*(1), 35–46.

Sarre, R. (1996). The Public, the Police and Australian Gun Policies. *Australian Journal of Forensic Sciences, 28*(1), 7–14.

Sarre, R. (1997). Crime Prevention and Police. In P. O'Malley & A. Sutton (Eds.), *Crime Prevention in Australia: Issues in Policy and Research* (pp. 64–83). Federation Press.

Sarre, R. (1999). Restorative Justice: Translating the Theory into Practice. *University of Notre Dame Australia Law Review, 1*(1), 11–25.

Sarre, R. (2000). Issues in Policing and Police Accountability. In R. Sarre & J. Tomaino (Eds.), *Considering Crime and Justice: Realities and Responses* (pp. 63–93). Crawford House Publishing.

Sarre, R. (2001). Beyond "What Works?": A 25 Year Jubilee Retrospective of Robert Martinson's Famous Article. *The Australian and New Zealand Journal of Criminology, 34*(1), 38–46.

Sarre, R. (2003). Some Thoughts on the Relationship Between Crime Prevention and Policing in Contemporary Australia. In S. P. Lab & D. K. Das (Eds.), *International Perspectives on Community Policing and Crime Prevention* (pp. 79–92). Prentice-Hall.

Sarre, R. (2004). The Future of Policing in a Broader Regulatory Framework. In R. Johnston & R. Sarre (Eds.), *Regulation: Enforcement and Compliance* (Research and Public Policy, no. 57, 77–90). Australian Institute of Criminology.

Sarre, R. (2008). The Legal Powers of Private Security Personnel: Some Policy Considerations and Legislative Options. *Law and Justice Journal, 8*(2), 301–313.

Sarre, R. (2009). The Importance of Political Will in the Imprisonment Debate. *Current Issues in Criminal Justice, 21*(1), 154–161.

Sarre, R. (2011). We Get the Crime We Deserve: Exploring the Disconnect in 'Law and Order' Politics. *James Cook University Law Journal, 18*, 144–161.

Sarre, R. (2012a). Police, Legitimacy and Crime Prevention: What Are the Intersections? *Australasian Policing: A Journal of Professional Practice and Research, 4*(2), 13–15.

Sarre, R. (2012b). The Threat of Imprisonment in the Battle Against White Collar Crime. In E. Pływaczewski (Ed.), *Current Problems of the Penal Law and Criminology* (5th ed., 615–625). Wolters Kluwer Polska.

Sarre, R. (2014). Legal Powers, Obligations and Immunities. In T. Prenzler (Ed.), *Professional Practice in Crime Prevention and Security Management* (pp. 149–161). Australian Academic Press.

Sarre, R. (2017). How I Would Spend $100 Million to Reduce Crime. *Current Issues in Criminal Justice, 28*(3), 339–353.

Sarre, R. (2019a, February 13). Yes, We Can Put Bank Bosses in Jail But Is that the Best Way to Hold Them to Account? *The Conversation.* https://theconversation.com/yes-we-can-put-bank-bosses-in-jail-but-is-that-the-best-way-to-hold-them-to-account-111507. Accessed February 2, 2024.

Sarre, R. (2019b). Gun Control: An Australian Perspective. In J. Carlson, K. Goss, & H. Shapira (Eds.), *Gun Studies: Interdisciplinary Approaches to Politics, Policy, and Practice* (pp. 177–195). Routledge.

Sarre, R. (2019c, March 21). Will the New Zealand Gun Law Changes Prevent Future Mass-shootings? *The Conversation.* https://theconversation.com/will-the-new-zealand-gun-law-changes-prevent-future-mass-shootings-113838. Accessed February 2, 2024.

Sarre, R. (2022). Policing Cybercrime: Is There a Role for the Private Sector? In J. Eterno, D. Petersen, & B. Stickle (Eds.), *Policing Contemporary Issues* (pp. 217–227). CRC Press.

Sarre, R. (2023). Perspectives on Policing Post-pandemic Cybercrime. In R. Smith, R. Sarre, L. Chang, & L. Lau (Eds.), *Cybercrime in the Pandemic Digital Age and Beyond* (pp. 173–192). Palgrave Macmillan.

Sarre, R., & Bartels, L. (2023, January 29). Discriminatory Impact on First Nations People: Coroner Calls for Urgent Bail Reform in Veronica Nelson Inquest. *The Conversation.* https://theconversation.com/discriminatory-impact-on-first-nations-people-coroner-calls-for-urgent-bail-reform-in-veronica-nelson-inquest-198507. Accessed January 30, 2024.

Sarre, R., Brooks, D., Smith, C., & Draper, R. (2014). Current and Emerging Technologies Employed to Abate Crime and to Promote Security. In B. Arrigo & H. Bersot (Eds.), *The Routledge Handbook of International Crime and Justice Studies* (pp. 327–349). Routledge.

Sarre, R., & Daly, K. (2021). Criminal Justice System: Aims and Processes. In D. Dalton, W. de Lint, & D. Palmer (Eds.), *Crime and Justice: A Guide to Criminology* (6th ed., 383–403). Thomson Reuters.

Sarre, R., Lau, L., & Chang, L. Y. C. (2018). Responding to Cybercrime: Current Trends. *Police Practice and Research: An International Journal, 19*(6), 515–518.

Sarre, R., & Prenzler, T. (2000). The Relationship Between Police and Private Security: Models and Future Directions. *International Journal of Comparative and Applied Criminal Justice, 24*(1), 91–113.

Sarre, R., & Prenzler, T. (2017). Privatisation in the Criminal Justice System. In D. Palmer, W. de Lint & D. Dalton (Eds.), *Crime and Justice: A Guide to Criminology* (5th ed., 427–444). Thomson Reuters.

Sarre, R., & Prenzler, T. (2018). Privatisation of Police: Themes from Australia. In A. Hucklesby & S. Lister (Eds.), *The Private Sector and Criminal Justice* (pp. 97–134). Palgrave Macmillan.

Sarre, R., & Prenzler, T. (2021a). Privatisation in the Criminal Justice System. In D. Palmer, W. de Lint, & D. Dalton (Eds.), *Crime and Justice: A Guide to Criminology* (6th ed., 455–473). Thomson Reuters.

Sarre, R., & Prenzler, T. (2021b). Policing and Security: Critiquing the Privatisation Agenda. In P. Birch, M. Kennedy, & E. Kruger (Eds.), *Australian Policing: Critical Issues in 21st Century Police Practice* (pp. 221–235). Oxford University Press.

Sarre, R., & Prenzler, T. (2023). Australian Public and Private Crime Prevention Partnerships in Cyberspace. In E. Blackstone, S. Hakim, & B. Meehan (Eds.), *Handbook on Public and Private Security* (pp. 85–102). Springer.

Sarre, R., & Richards, J. (2005). Responding to Culpable Corporate Behaviour: Current Developments in the Industrial Manslaughter Debate. *Flinders Journal of Law Reform*, *8*(1), 93–111.

Sarre, R., & Young, J. (2011). Christian Approaches to the Restorative Justice Movement: Observations on Scripture and Praxis. *Contemporary Justice Review*, *14*(3), 345–355.

Schneider, S. (2015). *Crime Prevention: Theory and Practice*. Routledge.

Segrave, M., Wilson, D., & Fitz-Gibbon, K. (2017, January 25). More Police Won't Necessarily Lead to Better Outcomes on Family Violence—Here's What We Need. *The Conversation*. https://theconversation.com/more-police-wont-necessarily-lead-to-better-outcomes-on-family-violence-heres-what-we-need-70755. Accessed January 31, 2024.

Sentencing Project. (2014). *Fewer Prisoners, Less Crime, A Tale of Three States*. https://www.sentencingproject.org/publications/fewer-prisoners-less-crime-a-tale-of-three-states/. Accessed 20 October 2023.

Serpell, B., Sullivan, T., & Doherty, L. (2022). *Homicide in Australia 2019–20* (Statistical Report No. 39). Australian Institute of Criminology.

Shaftoe, H. (2004). *Crime Prevention: Facts, Fallacies and the Future*. Palgrave Macmillan.

Shearing, C. (1989). Decriminalizing Criminology: Reflections on the Literal and Tropological Meaning of the Term. *Canadian Journal of Criminology*, *31*(2), 169–178.

Sherman, L., Gottfredson, D., MacKenzie, D., Eck, J., Reuter, P., & Bushway, S. (1997) *Preventing Crime: What Works, What Doesn't, What's Promising* (A Report to the United States Congress Prepared for the National Institute of Justice). Department of Criminology and Criminal Justice, University of Maryland.

Smith, R. (2017). Public Sector Criminological Research. In A. Deckert & R. Sarre (Eds.), *The Palgrave Handbook of Australian and New Zealand Criminology, Crime and Justice* (pp. 33–50). Palgrave Macmillan.

Smith, R. (2021). *The Changing Face of Criminology in Australia and New Zealand*. Sage.

Smith, R. (2023). *Public Sector Criminological Research: The Australian Institute of Criminology 1972–2022*. Palgrave Macmillan.

South Australia. (1989). *Together Against Crime: Policy Plan for the South Australian Crime Prevention Strategy*. Crime Prevention Policy Unit, Attorney-General's Department.

Stenning, P. (2009). Governance and Accountability in a Plural Policing Environment—The Story So Far. *Policing: A Journal of Policy and Practice*, *3*(1), 22–33.

Sutherland, E. (1949/1983). *White-Collar Crime: The Uncut Version*. Yale University Press (reprinted).

Sutton, A. (2000). Crime Prevention: A Viable Alternative to the Justice System? In D. Chappell & P. Wilson (Eds.), *Crime and the Criminal Justice System in Australia: 2000 and Beyond* (pp. 316–331). Butterworths.

Sutton, A., Cherney, A., & White, R. (2008). *Crime Prevention: Principles, Perspectives and Practices* (1st ed.). Cambridge University Press.

Sutton, A., Cherney, A., White, R., & Clancey, G. (2021). *Crime Prevention, Principles, Perspectives and Practices* (3rd ed.). Cambridge University Press.

Sutton, A., & Sarre, R. (1992). Monitoring the South Australian Cannabis Expiation Notice Initiative. *The Journal of Drug Issues, 22*(3), 579–590.

Sweeney, J., & Payne, J. (2011). *Alcohol And Disorderly Conduct On Friday And Saturday Nights: Findings From The DUMA Program* (Research in Practice Report no. 15). Australian Institute of Criminology. https://www.aic.gov.au/publications/rip/rip15. Accessed January 27, 2023.

Taylor, H., Bartels, L., Crowe, M., & Marshall, V. (2021). *Literature Review on Yarning Circles in a Criminal Justice Context*. Australian National University.

Teunissen, C., Boxall, H., & Napier, S. (2022). *The Sexual Exploitation of Australian Children on Dating Apps and Websites* (Trends and Issues in Crime and Criminal Justice, no. 658). Australian Institute of Criminology.

Thornton, D., Gunningham, N., & Kagan, R. (2005). General Deterrence and Corporate Environmental Behavior. *Law and Policy, 27*(2), 262–288.

Tilley, N. (2012). *Crime Prevention*. Routledge.

Tomasic, R. (2005). From White-Collar to Corporate Crime and Beyond. In D. Chappell & P. Wilson (Eds.), *Issues in Australian Crime and Criminal Justice*. LexisNexis Butterworths.

Tomasic, R. (2017). Exploring the Limits of Corporate Culture as a Regulatory Tool—The Case of Financial Institutions, 32. *Australian Journal of Corporate Law* 196.

Tomasic, R., & Dobinson, I. (1979). *The Failure of Imprisonment*. Allen & Unwin.

Tonry, M. (2011). Making Peace, Not Desert. *Criminology and Public Policy, 10*(3), 637–649.

Travers, M., Colvin, E., Bartkowiak-Théron, I., Sarre, R., Day, A., & Bond, C. (2020). *Rethinking Bail: Court Reform or Business as Usual?* Palgrave Macmillan.

Tubex, H., Brown, D., Freiberg, A., Sarre, R., & Gelb, K. (2015). Penal Diversity Within Australia. *Punishment and Society, 17*(3), 345–373.

Tyler, T., & Fagan, J. (2008). Legitimacy and Cooperation: Why Do People Help the Police Fight Crime in Their Communities? *Ohio State Journal of Criminal Law, 6*, 231–275.

United Nations. (2010). *Handbook on the United Nations Crime Prevention Guidelines*. United Nations Office on Drugs and Crime.

Van Dijk, J. (2008). *The World of Crime*. Sage.

Van Dijk, J., & de Waard, J. (1991). A Two-Dimensional Typology of Crime Prevention Projects. *Criminal Justice Abstracts, 23*(4), 483–503.

Van Kesteren, J. (2014). Revisiting the Gun Ownership and Violence Link: A Multi-level Analysis of Victimization Survey Data. *British Journal of Criminology, 54*(1), 53–70.

Van Steden, R., & Sarre, R. (2010). The Tragic Quality of Contract Guards: A Discussion of the Reach and Theory of Private Security in the World Today. *The Journal of Criminal Justice Research, 1*(1), 1–19.

Vinson, T. (1999). *Unequal in Life: The Distribution of Social Disadvantage in Victoria and New South Wales*. Jesuit Social Services.

Voce, I., & Morgan, A. (2023). *Online Behaviour, Life Stressors and Profit-Motivated Cybercrime Victimisation* (Trends and Issues in Crime and Criminal Justice, no. 675). Australian Institute of Criminology.

Vollaard, B. (2012). Preventing Crime Through Selective Incapacitation. *The Economic Journal, 123*(567), 262–284.

Wallace, A. (1986). *Homicide: The Social Reality*. NSW Bureau of Crime Statistics and Research.

Wan, W-Y., Moffatt, S., Jones, C., & Weatherburn, D. (2012). *The Effect of Arrest and Imprisonment on Crime* (Crime and Justice Bulletin, Report no. 158). NSW Bureau of Crime Statistics and Research.

Wan, W.-Y., & Weatherburn, D. (2022). Is Arrest for Prohibited Drug Use a Prelude to More Serious Offending? *Journal of Criminology, 55*(3), 322–337.

Waretini-Karena, R. (2017). Colonial Law, Dominant Discourses, and Intergenerational Trauma. In A. Deckert & R. Sarre (Eds.), *The Palgrave Handbook of Australian and New Zealand Criminology, Crime and Justice* (pp. 697–710). Palgrave Macmillan.

Weatherburn, D. (2009). Dilemmas in Harm Minimization: A Response to My Critics. *Addiction, 104*(3), 335–339.

Weatherburn, D. (2010). *The Effect of Prison on Adult Re-Offending* (Crime and Justice Bulletin, Report no. 143). NSW Bureau of Crime, Statistics and Research.

Weatherburn, D. (2014). The Pros and Cons of Prohibiting Drugs. *Australian and New Zealand Journal of Criminology, 47*(2), 176–189.

Weatherburn, D., Halstead, I., & Ramsey, S. (2016). The Great (Australian) Property Crime Decline. *Australian Journal of Social Issues, 51*(3), 257–278.

Weatherburn, D., & Lind, B. (1997). *Social and Economic Stress, Child Neglect and Juvenile Delinquency*. NSW Bureau of Crime Statistics and Research.

Weatherburn, D., & Lind, B. (1998). *Poverty, Parenting, Peers and Crime-Prone Neighbourhoods* (Trends and Issues in Crime and Criminal Justice, no. 85). Australian Institute of Criminology.

Weatherburn, D., & Ramsey, S. (2016) *What's Causing the Growth in Indigenous Imprisonment in NSW?* (Bureau Brief no. 118). NSW Bureau of Crime Statistics and Research.

Weatherburn, D., & Rahman, S. (2021). *The Vanishing Criminal: Causes of Decline in Australia's Crime Rate*. Melbourne University Press.

Welsh, B. C., & Farrington, D. P. (2012). *The Oxford Handbook on Crime Prevention*. Oxford University Press.

White, R. and Monod, S.W. (2017). Green Criminology, in A. Deckert and R. Sarre (Eds.) *The Palgrave Handbook of Australian and New Zealand Criminology, Crime and Justice*, 617–632. Basingstoke: Palgrave Macmillan.

Wickes, R., Ratnam, C., & Piquero, A. (2022). Welcoming Neighbourhoods: Place Attachment and Ethno-Racial Acceptance. *Journal of Immigrant and Refugee Studies*. https://doi.org/10.1080/15562948.2022.2128499

Wilkinson, R., & Pickett, K. (2009). *The Spirit Level: Why Greater Equality Makes Societies Stronger*. Allen Lane.

Wilson, E. (1983). *What Is to be Done About Violence Against Women?* Pengiun.

Winick, B., & Wexler, D. (2004). *Judging in a Therapeutic Key*. Carolina Academic Press.

Wortley, R., & Mazerolle, L. (Eds.). (2008). *Environmental Criminology and Crime Analysis*. Willan.

Wortley, R., & Prichard, J. (2023). Online Messaging as a Cybercrime Prevention Tool in the Post-pandemic Age. In R. Smith, R. Sarre, L. Chang, & L. Lau (Eds.), *Cybercrime in the Pandemic Digital Age and Beyond* (pp. 209–232). Palgrave Macmillan.

WSIPP. (2017). *Washington State Institute for Public Policy Website*. http://www.wsipp.wa.gov. Accessed January 27, 2023.

Index

A
Aboriginal courts, 52
Age of criminal responsibility, 55, 57, 69
Alcohol and crime, 64
Australian Capital Territory, 31, 57
Australian criminal justice system, 19, 22, 27, 61, 64, 71, 73
Australian Federal Police, 21
Australian Human Rights Commission, 23, 29
Australian Information Commissioner, 33, 38
Australian Parliament, 37, 39, 44, 62

B
Bail, 8, 12, 46

C
Child abuse and crime, 64
Child exploitation, xxiv
Child neglect and crime, 61, 64
Civil society, 23

Closed Circuit Television (CCTV), 2, 3, 22, 23, 34, 35
Community development, 11, 38, 43, 45, 47, 57
Corporate crime, 27, 28, 62
Corrections, 2, 3, 10, 12, 47, 50, 62, 67–69
Counter-productive effects, 8, 45
Counterterrorism, 21
Crime
  defining, 1
  drugs, 12, 36, 46, 47, 49, 56–58, 64
  international, 51
  organised, 12, 21, 37
Crime control, 8, 12, 15, 16, 23, 40, 44, 61, 62
Crime drop, 7, 9, 10
Crime Prevention Through Environmental Design (CPTED), xv
Crime rates, 7–10, 15, 16, 41, 46, 49, 55, 59, 63, 69, 70
Crime surveys, 8, 50, 64

Criminal negligence, 50
Criminogenic effects, 48, 56, 57
Criminological theory, 1, 3, 4, 28, 55, 56
Cultural approaches, 30, 59
Curfews, 18, 19
Cybercrime, 7, 8, 21–24, 33, 36, 37, 68
Cybercriminality, 8
Cyber-dependent crimes, 36
Cyber-enabled crime, 8, 36

D
Detention centres, 48, 69
Deterrence, 3, 27, 28, 31, 47, 48, 68
Deterrent effect, 2, 10, 29, 33, 48, 52, 62
Developmental criminology, 63
Digital world, 33, 38
Diversionary pathways, 68
Domestic violence, 2, 52, 58, 64
Drug crime, 12, 36, 46, 47, 49, 56–58, 64
Drunkenness, 12

E
Education, 3, 47, 50, 69, 70, 72
Electronic surveillance, 33, 34
Evaluations, 5, 6, 16, 40
Evidence-based research, 4, 5

F
Fear of crime, 56
Firearm licensing, 43, 68
First Nations peoples, 7, 19
Future challenges, 57

G
Globalisation, 34

Gun control, 12, 39, 43, 44, 62
Gun deaths, 41
Gun owner licensing, 39, 42, 62
Gun ownership, 40, 41
Gun registration, 39, 42

H
Hot spot policing, 17
Human rights, 51, 68, 70

I
Incarceration rates, 9, 46
Inequality, 11, 56, 63
Intelligence-led policing, 17
Intergenerational trauma, 17, 61, 63, 64

J
Justice reinvestment, 55, 58, 59

L
Legal powers, 68
Legitimacy theory, 15, 17

M
Media and crime, 34, 35
Mental illness, 17, 40, 49
Metadata retention, 37
Military-style weapons, 44
Mixed economy of policing, 23

N
National Committee on Violence (NCV), 43, 44, 72
New South Wales, 58
Northern Territory, 50, 57

O

Occupational crime, 28
Opportunity costs, 45, 47
Organised crime, 12, 21, 37
Over-representation, 19, 45, 48

P

Parole, 8, 12
Partnership policing, 23
Penal populism, 55
Personal crimes, 8
Police culture, 20
Police patrolling, 15, 17
Police performance, 16
Policymakers, 1, 3, 5, 6, 8, 52, 57, 61–63, 65, 67, 70
Policymaking, 5, 57, 59
Political imperatives, 44, 55, 56
Political will, 43, 73
Politicians, 55, 57, 60, 62, 67, 68
Post-release services, 47
Poverty, 20
Pre-release services, 68
Prisons, 10, 29, 45, 46, 48–52, 58, 68, 70, 71
Privacy, 35, 37, 38
Private partnerships, 22, 23
Private security, 2, 21–24, 34, 68
Proactive policing, 15–17
Probation, 12, 31, 45
Productivity Commission, 4, 7–9, 15, 16, 38, 45, 46, 48, 52
Property crime, 7, 10, 24
Prosecution, 2, 10, 12, 31, 62, 67–69
Punishment, 12, 24, 28, 31, 51
Punitive damages, 2

Q

Quality of life, 72
Queensland, 10, 52

R

Rational choice theory, 27, 28
Reactive policing, 15, 16
Recidivism, 10, 50
Regulation, 43
Rehabilitation, 45, 50–52, 55, 59
Restorative justice, 47, 68

S

SAPOL, 18
School failure and crime, 64
Sentencing, 12, 31, 46, 49, 51, 58
Sexual assault, 8, 46
Situational crime prevention, 3
Skills training, 69, 72
Social capital, 11, 24, 58
Social cohesion, 11
Social crime prevention, 3
Social disadvantage and crime, 63
Social inclusion, 11
Soft on crime, 47, 55
South Australia, 51, 57, 70
Street crime, 42
Surveillance, 3, 10, 33–35, 37, 62, 68

T

Technology, 23, 34–36
Terrorism, 23, 62
Third-party policing, 23

U

Ukases, 12, 68
United Kingdom, 29
United Nations, 9
United States, 9, 12, 16, 41, 47, 52, 64

V

Victims, 2, 18, 20, 31, 39, 42, 49, 51, 59, 68

Victoria, 49, 58
Violence against women, 7, 8

W
What works, 1, 5, 50, 61, 62
White-collar crime, 27–31
Whole-of-government approach, 2
Workplace violence, 28, 31, 42

Y
Youth justice, 47

Z
Zero sum game, 69

SPRINGER NATURE

GPSR Compliance

The European Union's (EU) General Product Safety Regulation (GPSR) is a set of rules that requires consumer products to be safe and our obligations to ensure this.

If you have any concerns about our products, you can contact us on ProductSafety@springernature.com

In case Publisher is established outside the EU, the EU authorized representative is:

Springer Nature Customer Service Center GmbH
Europaplatz 3
69115 Heidelberg, Germany

The manufacturer's authorised representative in the EU is Springer Nature Customer Service Centre GmbH, Europaplatz 3, 69115 Heidelberg, Germany. If you have any concerns regarding our products, please contact ProductSafety@springernature.com

Printed and bound by CPI Group (UK) Ltd, Croydon, CR0 4YY

26/03/2026

02078951-0003